COLLINS LONGMAN

Resource Atlas

Italy

CONTENTS

WITHDRAWN

Series Adviser   David Jones

In association with
The Geographical Association

First published 1993
Reprinted 1993, 1994, 1995
© Collins-Longman Atlases 1993

HarperCollins Publishers, PO Box, Glasgow G4 0NB
ISBN 0 00 360321 0

Longman Group UK Ltd., Longman House, Burnt Mill,
Harlow, Essex CM20 2JE
ISBN 0 582 21434 3

Printed in Hong Kong

JL 8562

The Roman Empire dominated Europe for five hundred years until it collapsed in AD486. In such a mountainous country strong local leaders and powerful neighbouring countries stopped Italy becoming one country again until 1887, when it was united by a leader called Garibaldi.

Today the regions of Italy have a strong sense of local identity and a developing interest in regional government that is underpinned by a language that has a variety of local dialects.

These issues are all highlighted within the atlas and the use of standard data allows pupils to make accurate comparisons between regions and the issues that are important to them at what ever level they are choosing for study.

This atlas looks at the contrasts between localities and regions in Italy, it includes photos, data and maps in a variety of scales.

Local place names have been used throughout. Some Italian place names have been corrupted into English eg. Firenze to Florence, just as London becomes Londra when corrupted into Italian. To be consistant local place names are used throughout.

The maps on this page explain three things:

The Italian Regions

European Community Regions used as a basis for the collection of standardized data

The location of five Italian regions chosen for detailed examination, these are Puglia, Piemonte, Toscana, Basilicata and Sardegna

European Community and Italian government data is used to provide a detailed picture of two localities (Siena and Milano) and the five regions specified above. Information is presented about all other regions, industry, social and environmental issues. This combination highlights the distinctive characteristics, regional variety and sense of identity of the country as a whole.

1. ITALIAN REGIONS

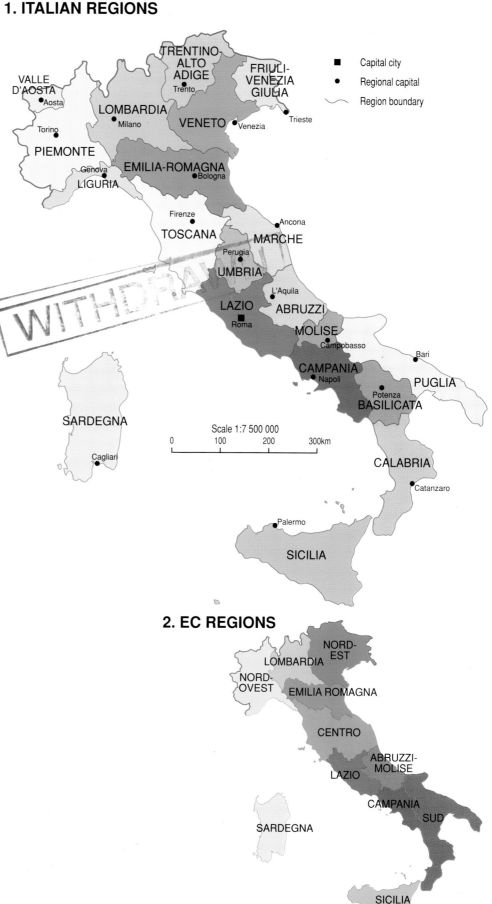

2. EC REGIONS

Locating Italy

Italy has a central position in Europe. The 1991 census recorded a population of 57,103,833 slightly higher than the UK.

Positioned between Europe and Africa, the country is surrounded by the warm Mediterranean Sea, that gives its name to the climate type. A founder member of the EC, Italy has a history that dates back beyond the Roman Empire.

To show the globe on a flat piece of paper geographers draw a grid to show the lines of latitude and longitude. This is called a projection and it will be centred on the area requiring greatest accuracy.

The lines of latitude and longitude on the globe converge at the poles. This is shown for the North Pole but Antarctica appears in two places because the projection has in effect cut up the globe and laid it flat. It is called a modified map.

1. THE WORLD

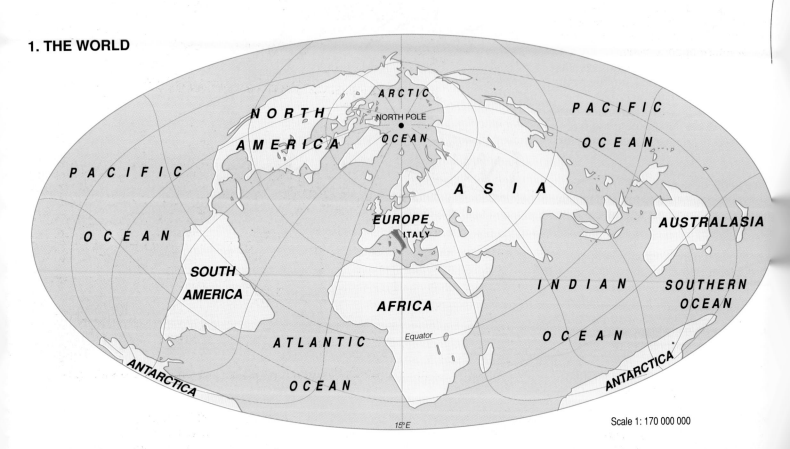

Scale 1: 170 000 000

The map above is a Euro-centric projection and the European land mass is the only truly accurate representation. The advantage of this map is that it gives an idea how far away other parts of the world appear to be to Italians.

Most British maps have the centre of the map on the Greenwich Meridian, 0° longitude. This world map is centred on the line of longitude 15° east and allows distance and direction to be estimated from Italy.

The map of Europe has changed a great deal recently. New countries are being created in eastern Europe and Italy is for many their nearest EC neighbour.

EC capital city place names are spelt in their native language.

Northern Italy has a border with France and is also close to southern Germany. This has encouraged the northern regions to seek more independence in their own affairs and look towards the EC for future opportunities.

2. EUROPEAN COMMUNITY (EC)

Italy
Other EC countries
Non EC countries
■ EC country capital

EC POPULATION 1992

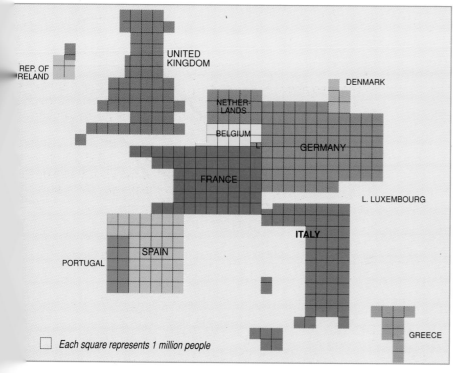

Each square represents 1 million people

The map to the left is a topologically transformed representation of the European Community. The transformation has tried to show the correct position of each country, but the size has been drawn by giving one square to represent one million of the country's population.

Italy had a population of just over 57 million at the 1991 census and so the size of the map is redrawn to scale.

Locating Italy 2

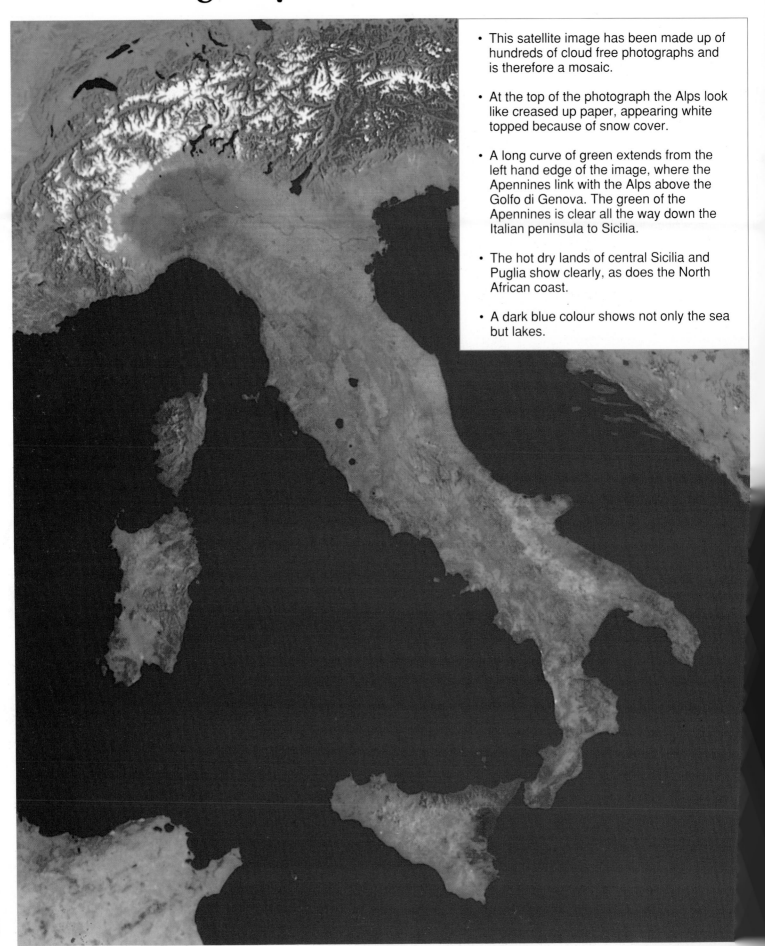

- This satellite image has been made up of hundreds of cloud free photographs and is therefore a mosaic.

- At the top of the photograph the Alps look like creased up paper, appearing white topped because of snow cover.

- A long curve of green extends from the left hand edge of the image, where the Apennines link with the Alps above the Golfo di Genova. The green of the Apennines is clear all the way down the Italian peninsula to Sicilia.

- The hot dry lands of central Sicilia and Puglia show clearly, as does the North African coast.

- A dark blue colour shows not only the sea but lakes.

This map shows the main physical features and major settlements of Italy. The Apennines dominate the country and can be seen on the satellite image opposite. Some cities, rivers and lakes can be found on both maps and satellite image. All place names are given their Italian spelling and a glossary is included below.

Height in metres
over 3000
2000 - 3000
1000 - 2000
500 - 1000
200 - 500
0 - 200

▲ mountain

● City or large town
○ Other town

Scale 1:5 250 000

0   100   200   300 km

Name Glossary

Italian	English
Dolomiti	Dolomites
Firenze	Florence
Genova	Genoa
Livorno	Leghorn
Milano	Milan
Napoli	Naples
Padova	Padua
Roma	Rome
Sardegna	Sardinia
Sicilia	Sicily
Tevere	Tiber
Torino	Turin
Venezia	Venice
Vesuvio	Vesuvius

Climate

- With its hot, dry summers and cool, wet winters, Italy experiences a Mediterranean climate.

- Altitude, distance from the sea and aspect give local weather variations.

- Winters are cold in the mountains

- The coasts are kept warm by the sea

- Winters from northern Europe spread south into Italy, bring snow to most mountains

- In summer, hot weather from Africa moves north to the whole country

1. PRECIPITATION AND WINDS

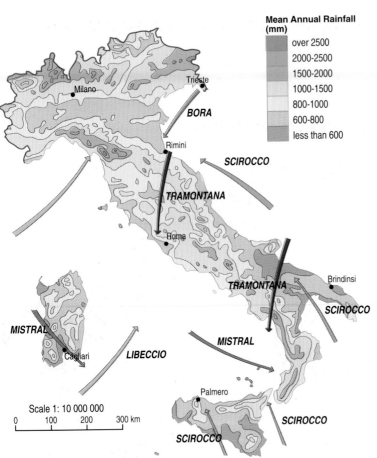

Mean Annual Rainfall (mm)
- over 2500
- 2000-2500
- 1500-2000
- 1000-1500
- 800-1000
- 600-800
- less than 600

The arrows on the map show the prevailing winds. In the winter these bring winter rain particularly to the mountains. Storms like the Mistral can bring snow and gales. Heavy thunderstorms bring the only summer rain and this rapidly evaporates. The Scirocco is a hot dry wind from Africa.

The graphs show how the Mediterranean climate has local variations. July temperatures are similar, but rainfall is lower in the south, and much lower in the summer than in the winter. Surrounded by warm seas and with mountains close by, the coast always has a breeze.

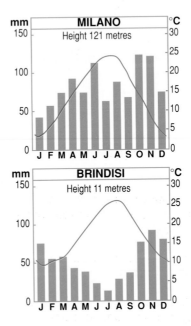

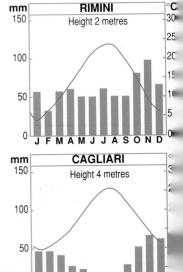

4. MANAGING SCARCE RESOURCES - Making good use of water supplies

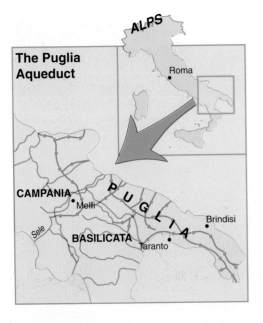

The Puglia Aqueduct

- The Puglia area is amongst the driest and hottest areas in Italy, and even in January temperatures average around 8°C.

- The largest aqueduct in Italy serves all of Puglia and much of Basilicata as well. The system of rivers, canals, pipelines and aqueducts starts from the river Sele in Campania and brings water to over 3 million people. It supplies most of the drinking water and some of the water for industry.

- Water condensed in the cooling towers of the power station is a source of fresh water that can be used in the steelworks in Taranto.

- All houses and hotels collect all rain water on their roofs and store it in underground tanks for use in swimming pools, washing and gardens. Some hotels purify this wa and add it to water from wells bored their grounds. This makes up the balance not brought by the aquedu but the water is often turned off for few hours a day in the summer to conserve supplies!

2. AVERAGE MONTHLY TEMPERATURE - January

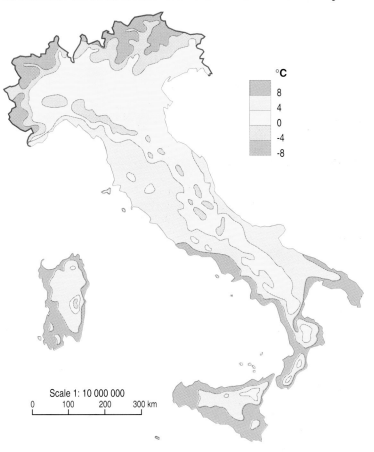

°C
8
4
0
-4
-8

Scale 1: 10 000 000
0   100   200   300 km

• Map 2 shows that warm winters are normal on the southern coasts. Temperatures drop quickly in the mountains.

• Winters in the north are much colder with a January average temperature of -8°C for alpine ski resorts.

3. AVERAGE MONTHLY TEMPERATURE - July

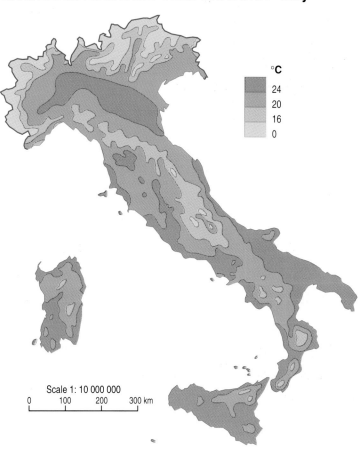

°C
24
20
16
0

Scale 1: 10 000 000
0   100   200   300 km

• Map 3 shows that large areas of Italy average 24°C all summer. The hot, dry Scirocco winds are short lived but can scorch crops and make life unpleasant.

Mountain areas are cooler with clear sunny skies. Hot air rising from the coasts brings thunderstorms.

The areas which experience the greatest change from summer to winter are the valleys of Toscana and Umbria.

Farmers grow a hard type of wheat which makes good bread and, more importantly, pasta, but needs less water. They sow it in the autumn to make the most of the winter rains and harvest it in early summer. Citrus fruits like oranges and lemons are grown in large gardens with date palms, fig trees and olive trees to provide shelter.

PROBLEM:-
• Shortage of water for all purposes
• Groundwater from wells unable to meet demand

CAUSE:-
• Limited summer and winter rain
• Long hours of sunshine
• High temperatures winter and summer

SOLUTION:-
• An aqueduct 2670 km long that supplies most drinking water
• Collection and storage of all available rain via roofs and underground cellars

Drawing water stored in the underground tank ▶

Natural Hazards 1

Forty million years ago violent earth movements pushed Africa into Europe.

These earth movements still produce earthquakes. The effect of earthquakes on some rocks *eg.* clay and marl, make some areas dangerous, as buildings collapse easily.

1. ROCK TYPES

2. MAJOR NATURAL DISASTERS 1951-1992

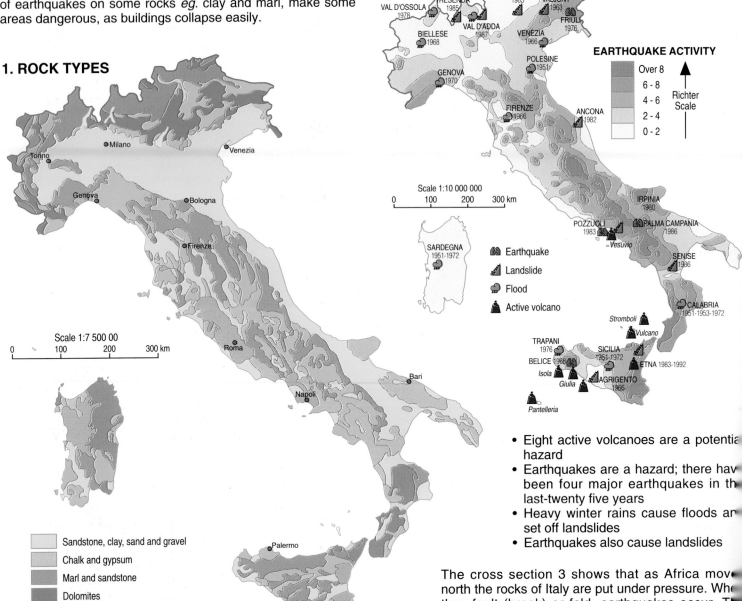

EARTHQUAKE ACTIVITY

Over 8
6 - 8
4 - 6   Richter
2 - 4   Scale
0 - 2

Scale 1:10 000 000
0   100   200   300 km

SARDEGNA
1951-1972

🫁 Earthquake
⛏ Landslide
☁ Flood
🌋 Active volcano

Scale 1:7 500 00
0   100   200   300 km

Sandstone, clay, sand and gravel
Chalk and gypsum
Marl and sandstone
Dolomites
Limestones
Mixed limestones and sandstones
Granites
Lavas
Other rocks

- Eight active volcanoes are a potenti hazard
- Earthquakes are a hazard; there hav been four major earthquakes in th last-twenty five years
- Heavy winter rains cause floods an set off landslides
- Earthquakes also cause landslides

The cross section 3 shows that as Africa mov north the rocks of Italy are put under pressure. Whe they fault (break) or fold, earthquakes occur. T heat generated by this movement melts the deepe rocks and this forms magma or volcanoes.

The folds can squeeze limestone into marble or tr oil, so the environment can be a resource and hazard.

3. AFRICA TO THE ALPS

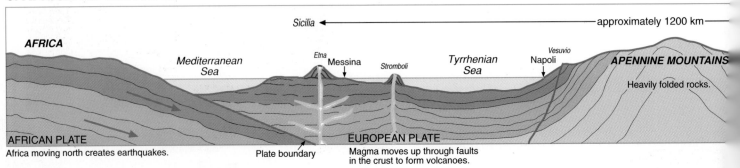

4A. MOUNT ETNA

- Reaching over 3000 metres Mt Etna is high enough to receive regular snowfalls.

- The steep sides and deep gullies show beneath the snow cover.

- A central magma chamber pushes hot lava up through rocks broken by earthquakes.

- Side cones, lava flows and ridges of ash cover the mountain side.

4B.

Ridges of ash

Mt. Etna main crater

Remains of old cone

Ridge of old lava flow

Side cone

New side cone develops as lava and gas push out of cracks caused by earthquakes

As lava cools, pipes feeding main crater and old cones become blocked

Hot molten rock and gas push upward through the mountain

Magma chamber

SOUTH   NORTH

Very old lava formed millions of years ago form the base of the mountain.

Recent lava flows form rich soils that attract farmers to work this dangerous land.

ɔt magma moves up through the ɔken rocks to form volcanoes. There ɛ no active ones north of Naples day, but granites and lavas show ɛre they use to be.

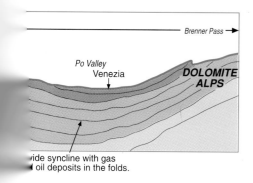

Brenner Pass →

Po Valley
Venezia

DOLOMITE ALPS

ide syncline with gas
d oil deposits in the folds.

4C.

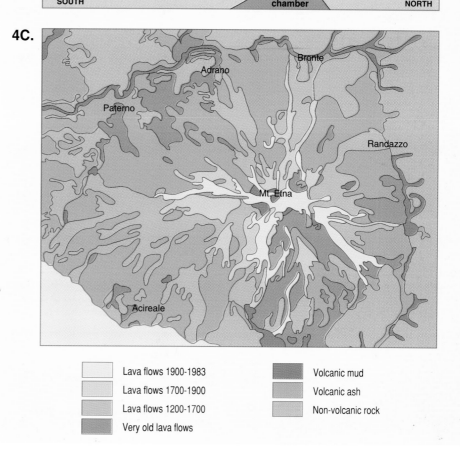

Bronte

Adrano

Paterno

Randazzo

Mt. Etna

Acireale

☐ Lava flows 1900-1983	☐ Volcanic mud
☐ Lava flows 1700-1900	☐ Volcanic ash
☐ Lava flows 1200-1700	☐ Non-volcanic rock
☐ Very old lava flows	

12 Natural Hazards 2

Napoli is one of Italy's four largest cities, just to the south is the Penisola Sorrento, one of Italy's major tourist areas.
The earth movements that made the Golfo di Napoli and the rocky peninsula, also made Vesuvio.
The physical environment can be a resource as well as a hazard.

- Napoli has grown up near Vesuvio as did the Roman town of Pompei.

- Napoli is one of the largest cities in Europe with the highest population density in Italy.

- The city has grown to dominate the Golfo di Napoli.

- The crowded city attracts people from the mountains of southern Italy.

- The rocky Penisola Sorrento to the south provides a beautiful setting for many of Italy's top hotels.

- This is a false colour Landsat image.

- The sea is almost black as are lakes and lagoons.

- The mountains and valleys show clearly like creased paper.
- These mountains run along the coast of the Penisola Sorrento.

- All of the hills and mountains have one side that appears to be darker. This is the shadow picked up by the satellite's cameras.

© Image Data Facility, DRA / Earth Ima

- The clear blue colour shows the built up area.

- Deeper blue shows the centre of towns and cities.

- Napoli harbour shows a pattern of pier, jetties and breakwaters.

- Find the lagoons (Lago) and the Volturno river.

- Look at the Landsat image and see how these appear.

- Vesuvio has a large main crater with a smaller central cone.

- Vesuvio destroyed Pompei in AD 79.

- The airport show clearly on Landsat image.

- The thin blue lines that join towns are roads and autostrada.

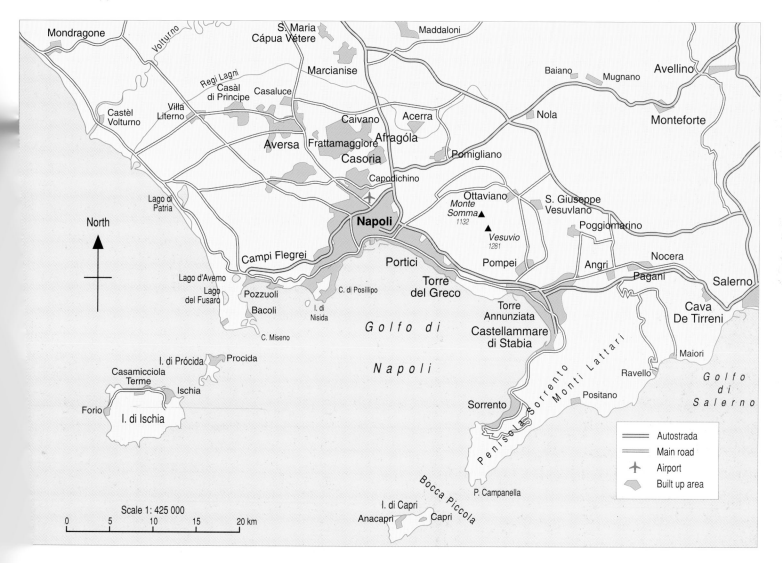

- North of Pozzuoli are many old volcanic craters.

- The town was destroyed by earthquake in 1983.

14 Environmental Issues

- The Mediterranean Sea is almost tideless, water flows in from the Atlantic Ocean to replace that lost by evaporation.

- Oil spilled by ships and waste discharged into rivers remain in the sea for long periods.

- A Blue Flag beach has a European standard of water quality.

- Protected land and National Parks are important to wildlife and natural vegetation.

- High mountain areas and woodlands that have survived in the hills help maintain the wildlife and air quality.

- Despite the long coastline, Italy has less protected coastal areas than France and the UK.

- Italy's percentage of land protected ranks in the bottom five of the EC.

- New tourist development areas are to be built on the coasts clear of oil pollution.

1. CONSERVATION AND POLLUTION

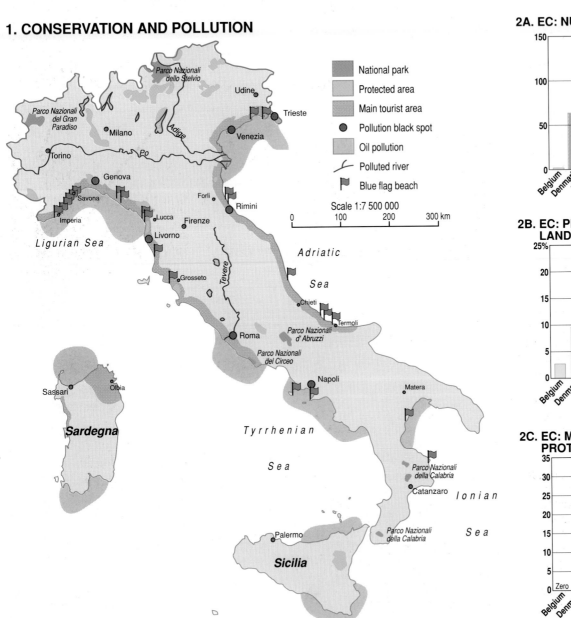

Legend:
- National park
- Protected area
- Main tourist area
- ● Pollution black spot
- Oil pollution
- Polluted river
- Blue flag beach

Scale 1:7 500 000
0   100   200   300 km

2A. EC: NUMBER OF PROTECTED AREAS

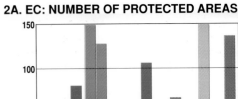
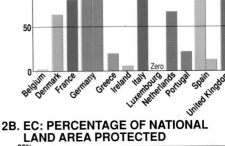

2B. EC: PERCENTAGE OF NATIONAL LAND AREA PROTECTED

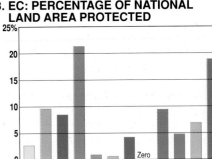

2C. EC: MARINE AND COASTAL PROTECTED AREAS

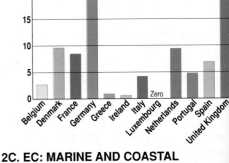
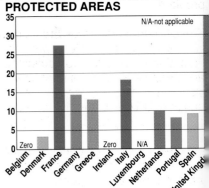

3. LAGUNA VENETA
(VENICE LAGOON)

- The satellite image of the Venice lagoon tells us a great deal about the hazards the city faces. To find the main harbour ocean going ships would use, follow the dark blue in from the sea and you can see where the deep water channels lie.

- The pinky/red patterns are sand and mud banks, and the greeny/blue is seaweed, growing on the mud banks in the shallower parts of the lagoon.

- From the farmland behind the lagoon, nitrates used as a fertiliser flow into the lagoon, and when mixed with the sewage effluent from the city causes seaweed to form floating banks of smelly vegetation over 20 metres long.

- The Adriatic Sea has a low tidal range, so pollution from large ships, the city and the farms stays close to the beach, encouraging a cloud of algae to drift down the coast.

- The coastal sand bars keep out the worst storms from the Adriatic sea, but the Bora winds blowing down from the mountains bring heavy rain, floods and rough seas right into the lagoon.

Built on wooden piles in the soft river mud of the Po delta, high tides and winter floods have always been a problem.

The city's famous canals are its roads, so every high tide or storm passes right alongside its famous buildings and peoples homes. As houses sink slowly into the mud, people move upstairs. Billions of Lira have been spent protecting famous buildings.

Land reclaimed from the lagoon for industry attract large ships whose wash damages the lagoon.

SPOT Image © CNES / NRSC / Earth Images

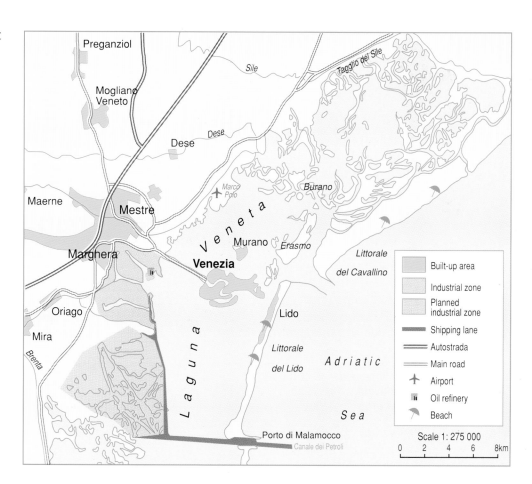

Population

1. POPULATION DENSITY

2. AREA AND POPULATION

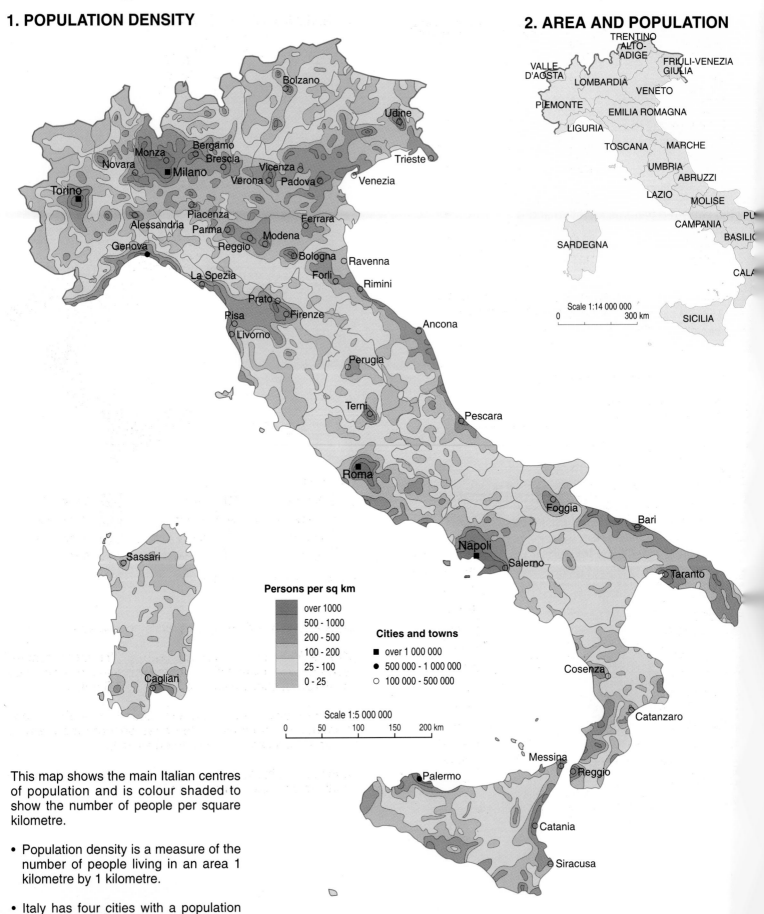

Persons per sq km

- over 1000
- 500 - 1000
- 200 - 500
- 100 - 200
- 25 - 100
- 0 - 25

Cities and towns
- ■ over 1 000 000
- ● 500 000 - 1 000 000
- ○ 100 000 - 500 000

Scale 1:5 000 000

0   50   100   150   200 km

Scale 1:14 000 000

0   300 km

This map shows the main Italian centres of population and is colour shaded to show the number of people per square kilometre.

- Population density is a measure of the number of people living in an area 1 kilometre by 1 kilometre.

- Italy has four cities with a population over one million, surrounding each is an area of high population density.

	Area (sq km)	Population (thousands)	Population Density (per sq km)
Piemonte	25398	4371	172
Valle d'Aosta	3262	114	35
Liguria	5417	1743	322
Lombardia	23858	8892	373
Trentino Alto-Adige	13618	883	65
Veneto	18363	4377	238
Fruili-Venezia Giulia	7845	1208	154
Emilia Romagna	22123	3922	177
Toscana	22992	3566	155
Umbria	8456	818	97
Marche	9693	1428	147
Lazio	17202	5146	299
Campania	13595	5752	423
Abruzzi	10794	1260	117
Molise	4437	334	75
Puglia	19347	4051	209
Basilicata	9992	622	62
Calabria	15080	2149	142
Sicilia	25707	5153	200
Sardegna	24089	1653	69

The table above shows an average population density for each region. The map shows where these people are concentrated in each region.

4. BIRTH RATES : DEATH RATES

■ Birth rate per 1000 people
■ Death rate per 1000 people

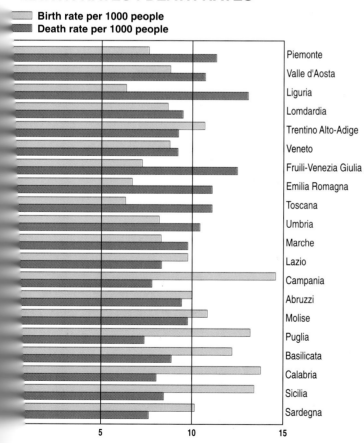

Piemonte
Valle d'Aosta
Liguria
Lomdardia
Trentino Alto-Adige
Veneto
Fruili-Venezia Giulia
Emilia Romagna
Toscana
Umbria
Marche
Lazio
Campania
Abruzzi
Molise
Puglia
Basilicata
Calabria
Sicilia
Sardegna

3. LANGUAGES AND DIALECTS

Scale 1:10 000 000
0   100   200   300 km

Languages

- Provenzale
- Franco-Provenzale
- Gaul Italic
- Venetian
- Ladino
- Tedesco
- Sloveno
- Toscano
- Mediano
- Mediano interno
- Mediano estremo
- Sardinian

The names on the map are local dialects eg. *Siciliano*

Italy is a country with many languages and dialects.

- The regions south of Toscana speak different languages, versions of Mediano Italian. Those areas to the north speak an Italian language related to French and German.

- People moved to the northern cities in search of work. Language and dialect differences encouraged many to return as soon as they had earned enough.

- Language differences are part of the tension between northern and southern regions of Italy.

Population and Migration

- The population is growing by at least 2.7% in those regions south of Umbria, except in Basilicata.

- The industrial regions of the north show slower population growth or an actual decline.

- Italians still move from the four most southerly regions, often to the central regions as well as the north. Tourism is helping Valle D'Aosta grow.

- Population Change is the growth or decline in the number of people. Internal Migration is movement to another Italian region.

- The movement of people from the Mezzogiorno to the industrial north was strongest before 1971.

- Now more service and industrial jobs available in the south.

1. POPULATION CHANGE

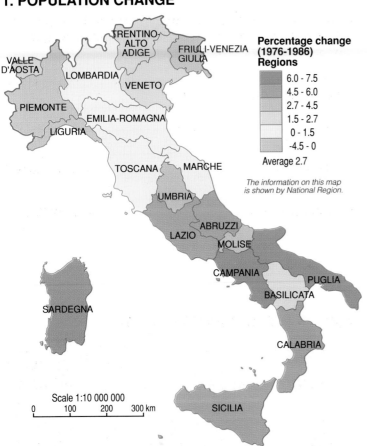

Percentage change (1976-1986) Regions

- 6.0 - 7.5
- 4.5 - 6.0
- 2.7 - 4.5
- 1.5 - 2.7
- 0 - 1.5
- -4.5 - 0

Average 2.7

The information on this map is shown by National Region.

Scale 1:10 000 000
0   100   200   300 km

3. INTERNAL MIGRATION

Migration Rate (per 1000 people)

- over 5
- 2.5 - 5
- 0 - 2.5
- -2.5 - 0
- -5 - -2.5

The information on this map is shown by National Region.

Scale 1:14 000 000
0   100   200   300   400 km

2. NORTH - SOUTH MIGRATION

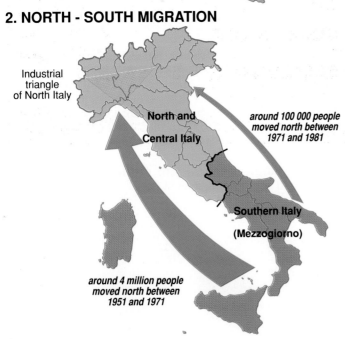

Industrial triangle of North Italy

North and Central Italy

around 100 000 people moved north between 1971 and 1981

Southern Italy (Mezzogiorno)

around 4 million people moved north between 1951 and 1971

4. EMIGRATION AND RE-ENTRY

More Italians have moved in search of a better life than most other Europeans. Many retire to their home regions or visit regularly throughout their life

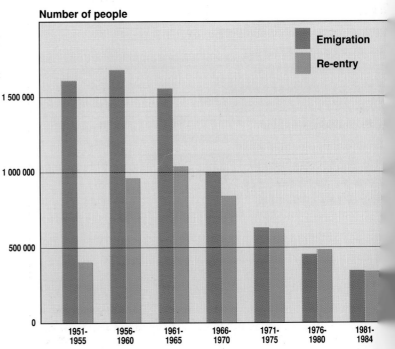

Number of people

Emigration
Re-entry

1951-1955 1956-1960 1961-1965 1966-1970 1971-1975 1976-1980 1981-1984

5. EMPLOYMENT STRUCTURE

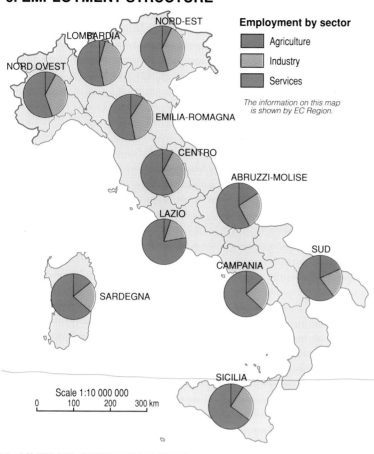

Employment by sector

- Agriculture
- Industry
- Services

The information on this map is shown by EC Region.

- Industry is most important in the central and northern regions.

- Agriculture is still important in the Mezzogiorno.

- Service sector employment includes tourist related jobs and accounts for over 50% of employment in each region.

- Eight regions have unemployment rates above the Italian average of 10%.

- Those regions with high unemployment are also those with the highest loss from migration. They are also the regions where agriculture is still important.

- Unemployment is lowest in Valle D'Aosta, the region where incoming migration is greatest.

- Italian unemployment is amongst the highest in Europe, but it has varied less than the United Kingdom.

- This consistent unemployment has contributed to the level of internal migration and external emigration.

- EC national unemployment has risen in the early 1990's.

6. UNEMPLOYMENT RATES

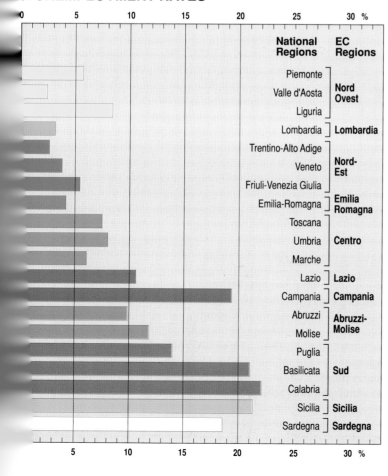

7. EC UNEMPLOYMENT RATES 1990

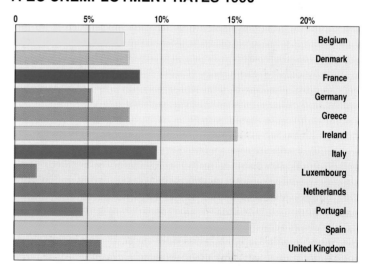

Economy

Italy is one of the seven richest nations in the world. Industry is still concentrated in the north.

Economic growth has been led by medium and low-tech manufacturing, such items as office equipment, electrical appliances, textiles, clothing and furnishings.

The "black economy" illegal business upon which no tax has been paid, is estimated at between 10 - 50% of the total GDP.

1. ECONOMIC ACTIVITY

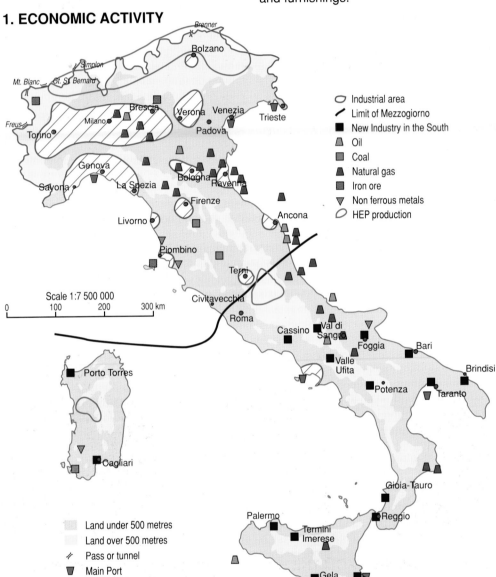

Industrial area
Limit of Mezzogiorno
New Industry in the South
Oil
Coal
Natural gas
Iron ore
Non ferrous metals
HEP production

Scale 1:7 500 000
0   100   200   300 km

Land under 500 metres
Land over 500 metres
Pass or tunnel
Main Port

3. GROSS DOMESTIC PRODUCT (GDP)

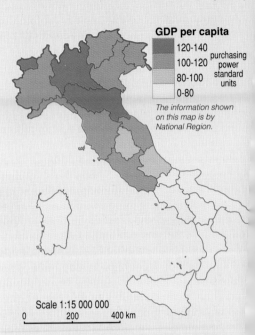

GDP per capita
120-140
100-120 purchasing power standard units
80-100
0-80

The information shown on this map is by National Region.

Scale 1:15 000 000
0   200   400 km

- Gross Domestic Product (GDP) is a measure of all the money earned by a region or a country, and is expressed as a value per head of population (per capita).

- The richest areas in Italy are still in the north, though EC and government investment has helped develop industry in the south.

- Italy's GDP compares well with other European and World economies, showing large scale growth up to the end of the 1980's. A rising national debt and government finances that are chaotic, pose problems for EC economic union.

GDP PER CAPITA 1989

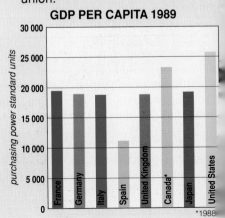

*1988

2. INDUSTRIAL PRODUCTION

CHANGE IN INDUSTRIAL PRODUCTION OVER PREVIOUS YEARS

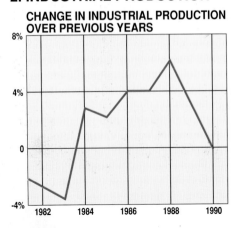

- Like most developed countries Italy's economy did well in the mid 1980's.

- The worldwide recession of the early 1990's has slowed growth in industrial production.

- The percentage employed in agriculture is higher than the national average in those regions within the Mezzogiorno.

- Those regions with the lowest GDP are found in the Mezzogiorno,

4. TRADE

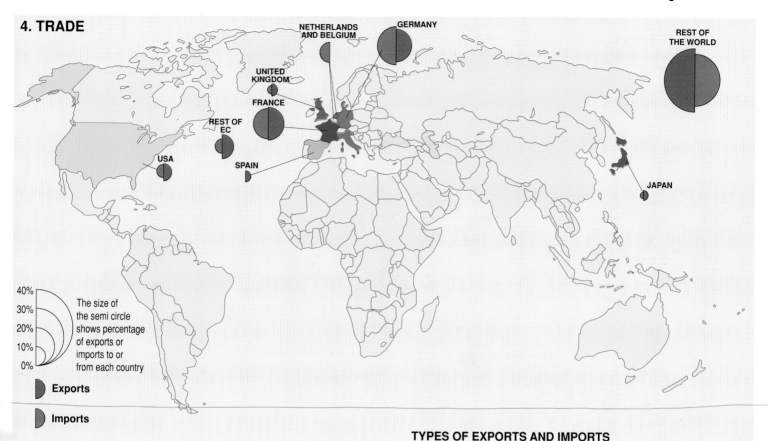

40%
30%
20%
10%
0%

The size of the semi circle shows percentage of exports or imports to or from each country

Exports

Imports

- Trade is what a country buys and sells.

- Exports are what a country produces and sells abroad.

- Imports are what a country buys abroad to use itself.

- Italy's major trading partners are EC countries, the USA and Japan.

TYPES OF EXPORTS AND IMPORTS

IMPORTS

8%
22%
12%
6%
15%
11%
13%
13%

Metal products and machinery

Textiles, clothing, shoes and furnishing

Transport equipment

Metals and other minerals

Chemicals

Agricultural and food products

Oil and coal products

Other

EXPORTS

12%
2%
7%
34%
8%
9%
10%
18%

5. REGIONAL AID FROM THE EC

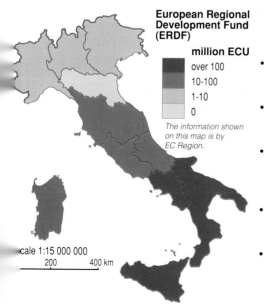

European Regional Development Fund (ERDF)

million ECU

over 100

10-100

1-10

0

The information shown on this map is by EC Region.

cale 1:15 000 000

200   400 km

- Italy has received a great deal of regional aid from the EC.

- Development money to help with new industry and infrastructure projects.

- The regions of the south have received grants to help with roads, industries and public services.

- Agricultural guarantees that help farmers.

- Guaranteed farm prices are an important part of the EC common agricultural policy, and help large numbers of small farmers.

TOTAL REGIONAL AID RECEIVED BY EC COUNTRIES 1987

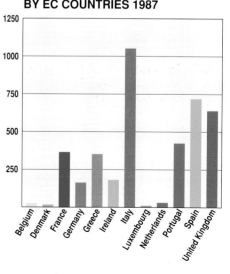

1250
1000
750
500
250

Belgium
Denmark
France
Germany
Greece
Ireland
Italy
Luxembourg
Netherlands
Portugal
Spain
United Kingdom

2. ROMAN ROADS

Via Iulia Augusta
Via Claudia Augusta
Via Fulvia
Via Postumia
Verona
Via Aurelia
Altinum
Augusta
Taurinorum
Genua
Via Aemilia
Via Postumia
Florentia
Via Aurelia
Via Cassia
Via Flaminia
Via Caecilia
Via Claudia
Valeria
Via Popilia
Via Aemilia
Roma
Via Valeria
Via Portuensis
Via Latina
Via Ostiensis
Via Appia
Via Saveriana
Via Traiana
Via Domitiana
Brundisiur
Neapolis
Tarentum
Via Hercilia
Messana
Via Valeria

Roman roads

Scale 1:10 000 000
0   100   200   300 km

1. LAND AND SEA TRANSPORT

To Austria
To Switzerland
Simplon
Tunnel
To Switzerland
Brenner Pass
A
L
P
S
Gt. St. Bernard Pass
To France
Aosta
Lt. St. Bernard Pass
To France
Freus Tunnel
Bolzano
Tirano
Trento
Udine
Como
Novara
Milano
Brescia
Vicenza
Treviso
Trieste
Torino
Verona
Padova
Venezia
Asti
Alessandria
Piacenza
Montova
Genova
Parma
Reggio
Modena
Ferrara
Savona
Bologna
Ravenna
La Spezia
Forlì
Rimini
San Remo
Massa
Prato
SAN MARINO
Imperia
Pisa
Firenze
To France
Livorno
Siena
To Western
Mediterranean
and America
Ancona
To Bastia
Pombino
Perugia
To Africa
Portoferraio
Elba
Terni
L'Aquila
Civitavecchia
Pescara
Roma
Termoli
La Maddelena
Frosinone
Campobasso
Foggia
Porto Torres
Sassari
Olbia
Gaeta
Bari
Alghero
Avelino
Napoli
Bosao
Orosei
Salerno
Potenza
Matera
Brindisi
Oristano
Arbatax
Lecce
Iglesias
Cagliari
Taranto
Porto
Foxi
Otranto
Pisciottao
Sepri
To Africa, Asia
and Australia
To Eastern
Mediterranean
Lipari Is.
Cosenza
Catanzaro
Trapani
Palermo
Milazzo
Messina
Mazara
del Vallo
Termini
Reggib
Enna
To Eastern
Mediterranean
Porto
Empedocieo
Agrigento
Catania
Vittoria
Siracusa
Modiga
Pantelleria

Scale 1:5 250 000
0   50   100   150   200

Autostrada
Main roads
Railway
Port
International shipping
National shipping
Land under 500 metres
Land over 500 metres

Italy's autostrada network has been built since 1950. A well engineered network of motorway standard roads, bridges and tunnels holds the country together economically and socially. For the cities of the north, movement over the border to the rest of Europe is easy, but without the autostrada, regions to the south would be cut off despite the many ports and ferry routes.

Many of the autostrada follow similar routes to the Roman roads. Land over 500 metres being a major influence even to modern road builders. The Romans did not build many roads over the Alps, but today tunnels allow traffic to move freely between the rest of Europe and the northern regions of Italy.

3. CAR OWNERSHIP
a: Selected EC countries

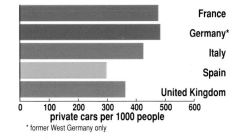

private cars per 1000 people
* former West Germany only

b. Italy by EC Region

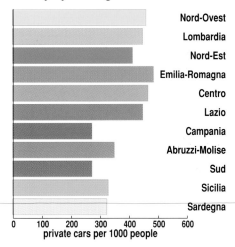

private cars per 1000 people

Italy is a major car owning economy, with higher numbers of private cars than the United Kingdom.

The development of the autostrada network has been important in encouraging Italians to travel within their own regions and to nearby large cities.

Many towns and cities have major traffic problems. Old narrow streets with important historic buildings are better for tourists than cars, so there are many bypasses (eg Siena, page 34/35), but cities do become solid with traffic at peak times.

4. AIR TRANSPORT

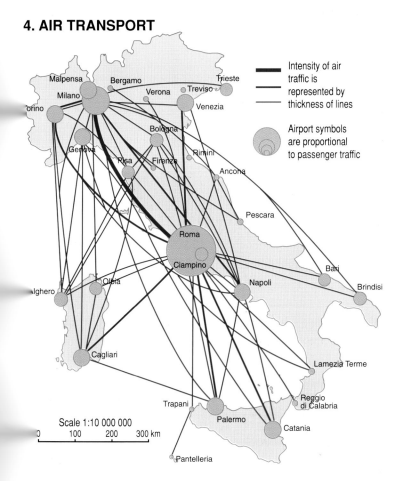

Intensity of air traffic is represented by thickness of lines

Airport symbols are proportional to passenger traffic

Scale 1:10 000 000
0   100   200   300 km

Roma is the major international airport, it is a "gateway city", one where you can change planes easily to travel onwards. Milano is a major European destination because of industry, but most other regional airports are small.

24 Agriculture

- Fruit and vines are grown in every Italian region.

- Almost 20% of the working population of the regions south of Abruzzi are employed in agriculture.

- East coast and southern regions have the highest percentage regional income from agriculture.

1. AGRICULTURE

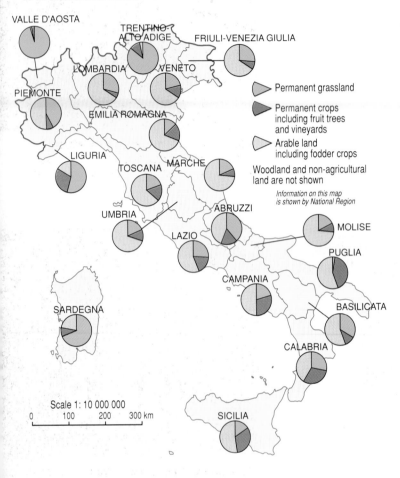

Permanent grassland

Permanent crops including fruit trees and vineyards

Arable land including fodder crops

Woodland and non-agricultural land are not shown

Information on this map is shown by National Region

Scale 1: 10 000 000
0   100   200   300 km

2. EMPLOYMENT IN AGRICULTURE

Percentage of workforce employed in agriculture

- 25 - 30
- 20 - 24
- 15 - 19
- 10 - 14
- 5 - 9
- 0 - 4

Information on this map is shown by National Region

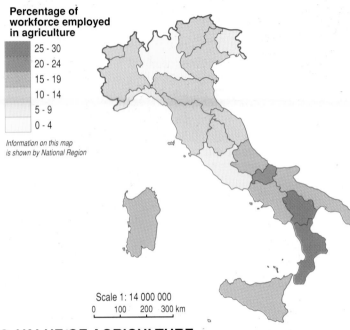

Scale 1: 14 000 000
0   100   200   300 km

3. VALUE OF AGRICULTURE

Percentage of Regional Income from Agriculture

- 8.1 - 10.0
- 6.1 - 8.0
- 4.1 - 6.0
- 2.1 - 4.0
- 0 - 2.0

Information on this map is shown by National Region

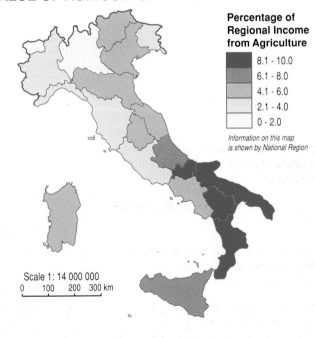

Scale 1: 14 000 000
0   100   200   300 km

The Italian countryside of Abruzzi is like so much of the country. Dotted with small farms and villages, but now with t. new autostrada nearby. Most farms are worked by families, some owning their farms, some renting from a landowner wl may not live in the area.

4. LAND USE

Woodland
Grassland/pasture
Arable
Irrigated land
Uncultivated land

Torino
Milano
Venezia
Genova
Bologna
Firenze
Roma
Bari
Napoli
Palermo

Scale 1: 7 500 000
0   100   200   300 km

Many farms have small fields growing crops closely together: salad vegetables like peppers for sale and maize to feed to chickens.

Tobacco is an important cash crop often grown in small fields and tended by hand.

Arable land will grow wheat suitable for pasta and maize as a fodder crop for animals.

Irrigated land in the north often grows rice.

Hills and mountains are covered in woodland, some is still used to produce charcoal.

Olive trees grown in groves are important as far north as Toscana, often providing shelter for other crops.

...ws of vines surround hundreds of ...all farms in almost every region.

Energy

- Italy depends on imports for 85% of her energy needs.

- Oil and natural gas are found on and offshore, but coal is limited.

- An extensive pipeline network moves oil and gas in northern regions and to Germany.

- Hydro-electric power (HEP) accounts for 13% of energy produced.

- A referendum closed all nuclear power stations in 1989.

- Geothermal power stations have been built in Toscana.

- Natural gas accounts for 63% of energy produced.

- Pipelines from Algeria, the ex USSR and the Netherlands bring gas.

- Oil brought by tanker is more than half the energy imported.

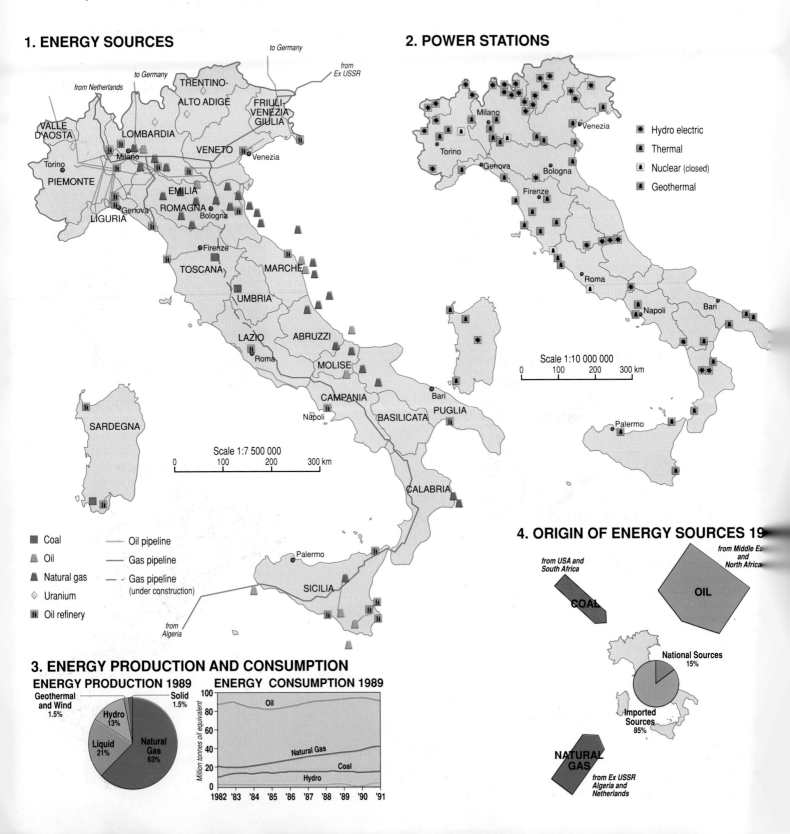

1. ENERGY SOURCES

to Germany
from Ex USSR
from Netherlands
to Germany

TRENTINO-ALTO ADIGE
FRIULI VENEZIA GIULIA
VALLE D'AOSTA
LOMBARDIA
VENETO
Venezia
Torino
PIEMONTE
Milano
EMILIA ROMAGNA
Genova
LIGURIA
Bologna
Firenze
TOSCANA
MARCHE
UMBRIA
LAZIO
ABRUZZI
Roma
MOLISE
CAMPANIA
Napoli
BASILICATA
PUGLIA
Bari
SARDEGNA
Palermo
SICILIA
CALABRIA
from Algeria

Scale 1:7 500 000
0   100   200   300 km

■ Coal
▲ Oil
▲ Natural gas
◇ Uranium
Ḟ Oil refinery

— Oil pipeline
— Gas pipeline
-- Gas pipeline (under construction)

2. POWER STATIONS

Milano
Venezia
Torino
Genova
Bologna
Firenze
Roma
Napoli
Bari
Palermo

✳ Hydro electric
▣ Thermal
▲ Nuclear (closed)
▪ Geothermal

Scale 1:10 000 000
0   100   200   300 km

3. ENERGY PRODUCTION AND CONSUMPTION

ENERGY PRODUCTION 1989

Geothermal and Wind 1.5%
Solid 1.5%
Hydro 13%
Liquid 21%
Natural Gas 63%

ENERGY CONSUMPTION 1989

Million tonnes oil equivalent
100
80
60
40
20
0

Oil
Natural Gas
Coal
Hydro

1982 '83 '84 '85 '86 '87 '88 '89 '90 '91

4. ORIGIN OF ENERGY SOURCES 19

from USA and South Africa
COAL

from Middle Ea and North Africa
OIL

National Sources 15%
Imported Sources 85%

NATURAL GAS
from Ex USSR Algeria and Netherlands

5. WEALTH CREATION

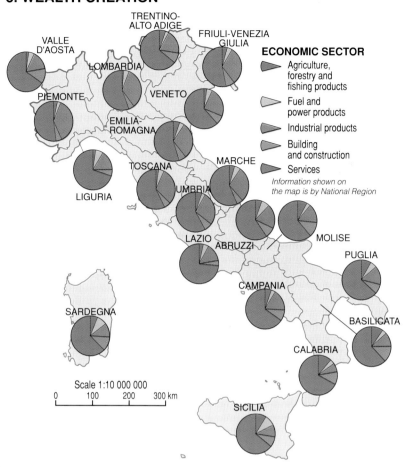

ECONOMIC SECTOR

- Agriculture, forestry and fishing products
- Fuel and power products
- Industrial products
- Building and construction
- Services

Information shown on the map is by National Region

Scale 1:10 000 000
0   100   200   300 km

- The service sector provides more than 50% of the wealth generated in all regions.

- Industry creates more wealth than agriculture in every region except Calabria.

- 9% of Italians are employed in agriculture.

- Employment in manufacturing has declined in the north and increased in Abruzzi and Molise.

- Service sector employment has grown in every region.

8. MANUFACTURING INDUSTRY

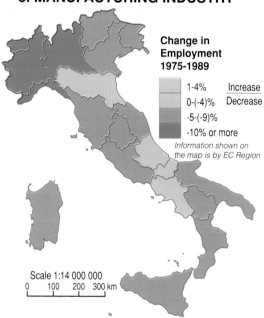

Change in Employment 1975-1989

- 1-4%   Increase
- 0-(-4)% Decrease
- -5-(-9)%
- -10% or more

Information shown on the map is by EC Region

Scale 1:14 000 000
0   100   200   300 km

6. EMPLOYEES BY ECONOMIC SECTOR

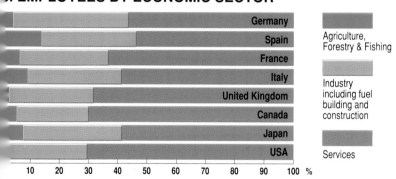

Germany
Spain
France
Italy
United Kingdom
Canada
Japan
USA

10 20 30 40 50 60 70 80 90 100 %

- Agriculture, Forestry & Fishing
- Industry including fuel building and construction
- Services

7. TOP 10 ITALIAN COMPANIES

Company	Products	Number of Employees
IRI-Istituto per la Riconstruzione Industriale	Telecommunications, steel and other industry	366 694
Fiat Sp A	Transport	286 294
ENI-Ente Nazionale Idrocarburi	Oil, gas and chemicals	82 748
Ferruzzi Finanziaria Sp A	Chemicals, pharmacceuticals, edible oils	44 546
Pirelli Sp A	Rubber products, cables	69 239
Olivetti C (Ing.C)	Business machinery and system manufacture	56 937
IBM Italia Sp A	Electronics	14 228
Esso Italiana Sp A	Oil	2 289
Rinascente (La) Sp A	Stores	14 187
API Anonima Petroli Italiana Sp A	Oil	not available

9. SERVICE INDUSTRY

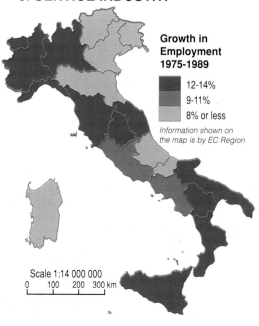

Growth in Employment 1975-1989

- 12-14%
- 9-11%
- 8% or less

Information shown on the map is by EC Region

Scale 1:14 000 000
0   100   200   300 km

The Textile Industry

The textile and clothing industry is the oldest in Italy, found in large cities and small market towns. The industry is more important in terms of employment to Italy than to other EC nations. Completely redeveloped by 1960, it generates 18,400 billion lira p.a. It has four main centres:

- **Milano** and the northwest, where cotton, linen and hemp helped develop the clothing industry which today employs over 160,000 people.

- **Toscana** has a large number of clothing and leather tanning companies with large scale production centres at Prato and Arezzo, employing nearly 60,000 people.

- **Marche,** the villages of the Adriatic coast have a reputation for high quality clothing and footwear, and employ 18,000 people.

- **Napoli** has specialised in footwear and garment manufacturing, where low cost operations employs 33,000 people.

1. EC TEXTILE INDUSTRY

Textile Industry Employees 1989

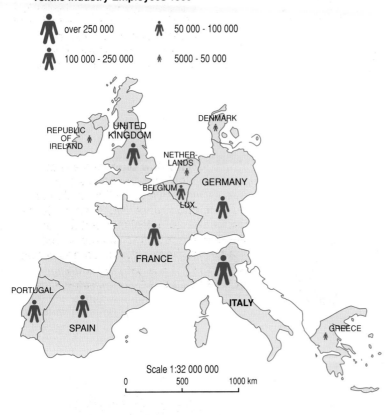

over 250 000

100 000 - 250 000

50 000 - 100 000

5000 - 50 000

Scale 1:32 000 000

0   500   1000 km

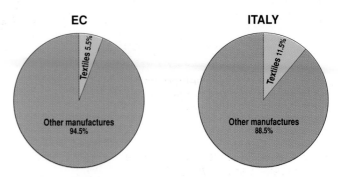

The graphs show people employed in the textile industry as a percentage of all people employed in manufacturing.

- The employment, exports and turnover of the Italian textile, clothing and footwear industries make it the country's largest industry.

- It is lead by family owned firms with international reputations, like the Marzotto group.

- The group has 20,000 customers, operates in 62 foreign countries, has 30 plants, 13,000 employees and offices in USA, Germany and France - its three major foreign markets.

- Specializing in fashion design and fabrics, the company has been a family run business for 118 years.

- Links with major Italian fashion houses like Ferre and Missoni enable its products to feature in the Milan fashion show each year.

2. TEXTILE INDUSTRY IN ITALY

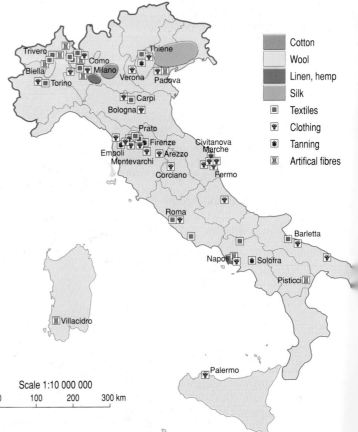

Cotton

Wool

Linen, hemp

Silk

▥ Textiles

♈ Clothing

◉ Tanning

▨ Artifical fibres

Scale 1:10 000 000

0   100   200   300 km

Fara d'Adda, water power helped start the woollen industry. Many of Italy's factories have their own hydro electric plants.

Schio, modern, highly automated factories need space to layout large scale machines and access to roads.

The Marzotto group's first factories were in Valdagno near Verona. A family run firm with a strong commitment to its work force; housing, schools and good working conditions were developed along with the latest technology.

In the 1970's, by constant investment, the group had continued to grow by buying companies with overseas markets or production it needed.

During the 1980's the group expanded by buying Basetti, one of Italy's most important textile companies. Other takeovers allowed Marzotto to become a leading linen producer.

The company now produces a wide range of wool, cotton and linen cloth and an extensive collection of clothes for men and women. Suits, shirts, jeans, sportswear and designer clothes for some of the most fashion conscious markets in the world. The company that started with 12 employees, now generates sales of 812 million lira.

30 Car Industry

- The car industry is often considered a good indicator of a country's prosperity, the greater the sales, the better a country's economy and particularly employment figures. In Italy this prosperity is generated by the Fiat group.

- Vehicles produced within the EC can be sold anywhere within the community without tariff (tax) barriers. Those made outside the EC are subject to sales quotas. This has encouraged Japanese firms to set up manufacturing plants in Europe, but Fiat have been able to prevent this development in Italy.

- The Italian car industry is Fiat, all the important brand names such as Lancia, Ferrari, Maserati and Alfa Romeo are all linked with or owned by the company.

- Originally based in Torino, the company now has plants all over the country and challenges Volkswagen as the largest single car producer in Europe.

- One of the largest industrial companies in the world, it employs 288,500 people, generating 50,241 million US dollars in 1991.

- The importance of the Fiat group to the European car industry is that it dominates Italian production and is not controlled by foreign companies.

Fiat works with or owns companies in other countries, making 21% of the cars sold in Brazil. Cars in kit form for local assembly are sold to Argentina, Venezuela and Turkey. The IVECO range is jointly owned with Ford and built all over Europe as well as under licence in China and Iran. Producing farming equipment with John Deere, construction plant with Hitachi, the Fiat group has diversified into civil engineering, chemicals, aircraft engines, component manufacturing, financial services and railway systems.

1. EC CAR INDUSTRY
Vehicle Production 1991

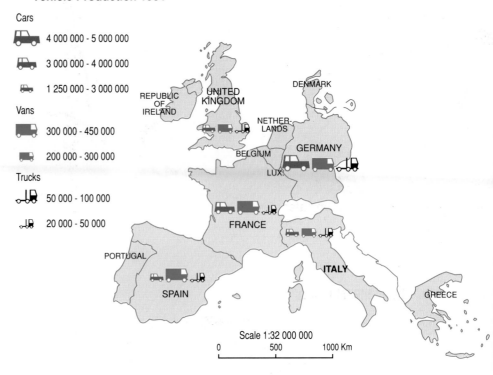

2. FIAT OPERATIONS

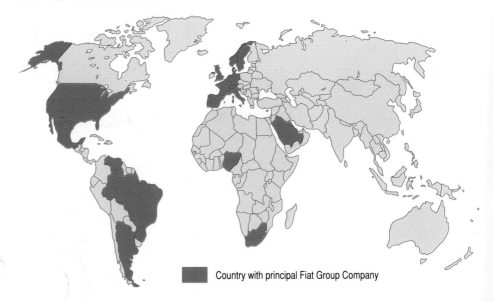

Country with principal Fiat Group Company

The huge Miraflori factory dominates Torino.
60% of the city's jobs depend on Fiat.
Company flats near the factory house migrant workers.

The new bodywork factory at Cassino produces panels for mid-range saloon cars. Built on flat land along side the autostrada to Roma.

3. FIAT FACTORIES IN ITALY

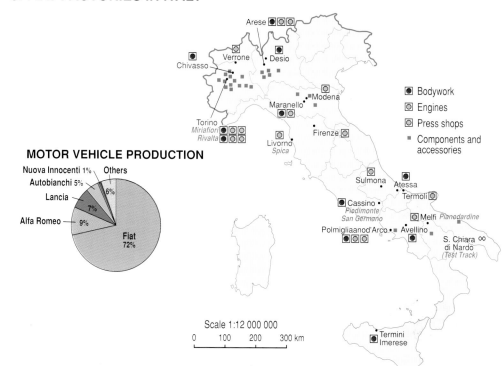

Legend:
- ◉ Bodywork
- ◎ Engines
- ▣ Press shops
- ■ Components and accessories

Map labels: Arese, Verrone, Chivasso, Desio, Modena, Maranello, Torino Miriafiori Rivalta, Livorno Spica, Firenze, Sulmona, Atessa, Termoli, Cassino Piedimonte San Germano, Melfi Pianodardine, Polmigliaanod'Arco, Avellino, S. Chiara di Nardo (Test Track), Termini Imerese

Scale 1:12 000 000
0   100   200   300 km

MOTOR VEHICLE PRODUCTION

Pie chart:
- Nuova Innocenti 1%
- Others 6%
- Autobianchi 5%
- Lancia 7%
- Alfa Romeo 9%
- Fiat 72%

Fiat has spread its motor vehicle plants throughout Italy. Originally based in Torino, the company has developed new factories on greenfield sites. Where ever low cost locations and financial help has been available the company has been prepared to build a factory providing there is access to the autostrada or a port.

Some factories produce complete cars but others concentrate on engines or parts, these components are then moved by road to other factories.

As the company owns other major brand names like Lancia, component parts and development costs are shared with the final badge being applied at the assembly plant.

rand new factory at Melfi, where a highly automatic plant build the Fiat Uno.

"Sunshine, beaches, warm seas, famous cities and more history than most people can remember." This is not a quote from a holiday brochure, but a comment from a 16 year old pupil returning from an exchange programme. Add to this mountains, volcanoes, lakes, glaciers and islands then you can begin to understand what natural advantages Italy has for the development of the holiday industry.

Since Europeans started taking holidays, Roma, Pisa, Venezia and Firenze have been an attraction, originally to the rich, but more recently to everybody. A country rich in history, having weather good enough to allow you to enjoy looking at it outdoors was almost bound to become a major tourist destination.

Employment in the service sector means providing services, working in hotels, restaurants, shops or in an entertainment facility. This type of employment accounts for over half of the jobs available in every Italian region.

The map shows the major coastal, mountain and lake resorts, holidays at these venues often encourage tourists to visit local or national cultural resorts.

Tourist development areas have been set up by the government to provide facilities, such as roads and hotels in some quiet but beautiful areas.

1. TOURIST CENTRES

Legend:
- ☀ Coast and lake resorts
- ▣ Cultural resorts
- ⛰ Mountain resorts
- ▨ Spa's
- ● Other cities
- Riviera
- Tourist development area

Scale 1:7 500 000
0   100   200   300 km

2a. ORIGIN OF TOURISTS

Germans are the major tourist group, but Italy's immediate neighbours account for another 22%. Visitors from the former communist countries and Japan are some of those included in the 'Others' categories.

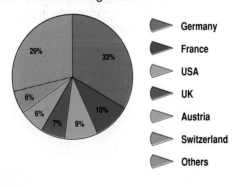

- Germany — 33%
- France — 10%
- USA — 9%
- UK — 7%
- Austria — 6%
- Switzerland — 6%
- Others — 29%

2b. NUMBERS OF VISITORS

Despite the competition from other major tourist destinations eg USA, Spain or France, Italy's total number of visitors has continued to rise.

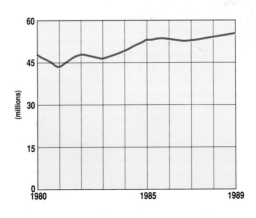

(millions)
60, 45, 30, 15, 0
1980   1985   1989

2c. TOURIST RECEIPTS

With earnings of over 12,000 million U dollars per year, tourism is vital to Italy New tourist development areas will he to 'attract more visitors'.

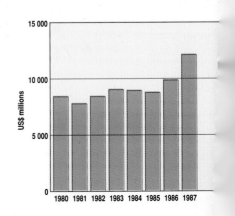

US$ millions
15 000, 10 000, 5 000, 0
1980 1981 1982 1983 1984 1985 1986 1987

Accommodation and Board	De France HB		
Number of Nights	7	14	14
	AIR	AIR	RAIL
Departure Days		Sun	Sat
30 May - 5 Jun	363	534	673
6 Jun - 12 Jun	384	559	692
13 Jun - 26 Jun	387	566	699
27 Jun - 10 Jul	436	659	779
11 Jul - 17 Jul	445	692	839
18 Jul - 24 Jul	464	719	839
25 Jul - 14 Aug	505	779	889
15 Aug - 21 Aug	492	656	809
22 Aug - 28 Aug	406	586	726
29 Aug - 4 Sep	398	559	699

(Left column label: DEPARTURE ON OR BETWEEN)

Supplements per person per night Suite for 4 persons £12.50

Accommodation and Board	Capo Boi FB	
Number of Nights	7	14
	AIR	AIR
30 May - 5 Jun	518	814
6 Jun - 12 Jun	518	823
13 Jun - 19 Jun	542	888
20 Jun - 26 Jun	542	975
27 Jun - 3 Jul	642	1099
4 Jul - 10 Jul	644	1129
11 Jul - 17 Jul	692	1189
18 Jul - 24 Jul	737	1219
25 Jul - 31 Jul	737	1238
1 Aug - 7 Aug	749	1195

(Left column label: DEPARTURE ON OR BETWEEN)

Children's Reductions
- sharing a room with 2 full fare paying adults.
Departure date
- 30 May 70% Reduction
- 1 Aug 30% Reduction
All prices are per person

Rimini, at the heart of the Adriatic Riviera is famous for its 16 kilometres of beaches. Average summer temperatures in July are above 30°C with over 10 hours of sunshine. Described in the brochures as "famed for its fine hotels, excellent water sports and bright night-spots, with the modern glamour of a lively seafront".

Cagliari is the capital and main port of Sardegna. On the south coast of the island is the Capo Boi hotel. The airport is a 50 kilometre drive from the resort. Set on a private beach at the end of a wooded valley this hotel complex aims to provide everything you could want for a "really lazy sun and beach holiday". The advertisements suggest that people come for the peace and quiet, the range of sports facilities, tennis to windsurfing and good food. Prices favour the family with young children.

All prices are in £ per person per night in two bedded room

	Europeo	Corona	Vidi
07.01.92 13.02.92	42	40	35
14.02.92 15.03.92	37	35	30
21.12.91 06.01.92	60	50	40

Pinzolo , 210 km from Milano, in an alpine valley, this village and those nearby, provide high quality ski facilities during four months of the year.
Over 200 km of ski runs are served by 30 ski lifts and 54 hotels. Skating, climbing, hang gliding, swimming and artificial snow machines, help extend the holiday.

Siena

The warm Mediterranean climate and good soils make farming a major local industry, with salad crops, tobacco and fruit important.
The countryside all around Siena is dotted with small farming villages, usually on easily defended hill top sides.

Siena, the street pattern within the town walls is narrow and unsuited to traffic. The large public plazas need protection and the local council refuse to allow changes or developments that would endanger the nature of the old town.

Built on three hills over 300 metres above sea level, Siena is a classic Italian hilltop town. The layout of the town still reflects its history. The town walls are still almost intact, and were developed between the 12th and the 15th century when the struggle with Firenze for control of Toscana reached a peak.

Farming is still very important as is wine making. Pharmaceutical and confectionary firms take local agricultural products to make health foods, medicines and sweets. Tourism relies on the city's history to attract large numbers of visitors each year. Banking has survived from the Middle Ages and is internationally important.

1. SIENA

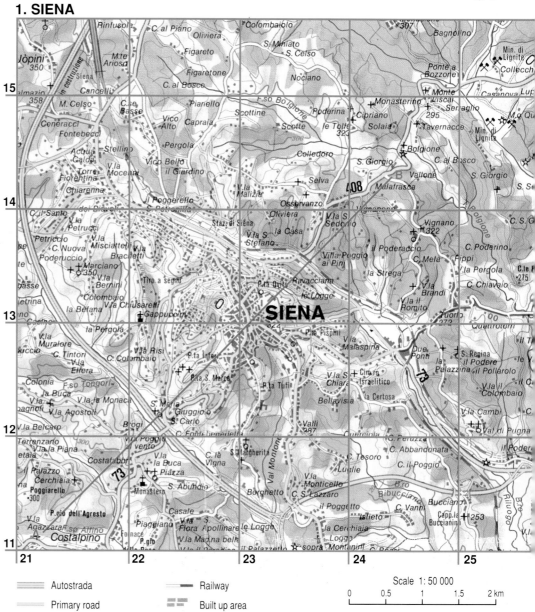

The autostrada arrives from the north, most main towns would have welcomed this, but Siena insisted that the road bypassed to the west. The reasons for this are given on page 34, but the decision made building the road easier.

Compare the route taken by the railway when it was built nearly a hundred years ago, with that of the autostrada now under construction. Siena has developed north west along the railway line. Small villages between Siena and the autostrada may become part of an enlarged town.

The number of villages indicates that the farmland is still rich and productive, most are built on hilltop sites surrounded by the fields they depend upon.

Autostrada	Railway
Primary road	Built up area

Scale 1:50 000

0   0.5   1   1.5   2 km

Not all symbols on the map appear in the key.

© Heinz Fleischmann GmbH u. Co. Geographischer Verlag D-8130 Starnberg

2. CROSS SECTION A-B

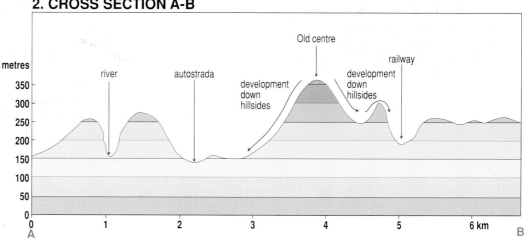

The cross section drawn from the map between points **A** and **B** shows the relief of the area and how this affects land use.

The original route for the autostrada would have closely followed the railway cutting through the eastern side of Siena.

Roads and railways have difficulty making straight lines between two places because of relief. The river valleys are natural routeways.

Milano

The economic capital of Italy, Milano is part of a conurbation of over 3 million people. The city dominates the Lombardia region which is both a national and EC region.

1. GROWTH OF MILAN

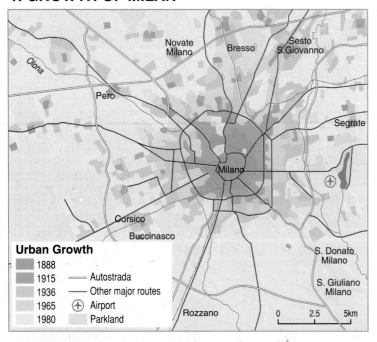

Urban Growth
- 1888
- 1915 — Autostrada
- 1936 — Other major routes
- 1965 ⊕ Airport
- 1980 ▨ Parkland

0   2.5   5km

From its old historic centre, Milano has grown steadily and has a succession of ring roads built as the city expanded. Autostrada also circle the city whose industry and financial strength dominates Italy.

Between World War 1 and World War 2, the city's expansion began to absorb nearby towns. Since 1980 the city has grown to almost fill the area of the outer autostrada ring road past the airport to the east.

The satellite image on page 6 shows Milano, its suburbs and commuter towns stretching as far north as lake Como.

- Milano leads Italian industry, dominating even its near neighbour Torino.

- Based in the city are E.N.I. (oil, gas and chemicals), Alfa Romeo, part of the Fiat group, Pirelli the tyre company as well as Autobianchi and Innocenti the motorcycle manufacturers.

- This dominance of heavy industry produced not only large companies but hundreds of small engineering and component firms as well.

- Despite the importance of industry, over 60% of the active population are involved in the service sector with banks, finance and insurance companies, and the Borsa - Italy's main stock market.

- Clothing and the fashion industry employs over 120,000 in the city. Many of these work for major names in the industry such as Benetton, Versance, Armani and Gucci. These companies operations in the city have hundreds of small workshops producing clothes of the finest quality.

- Like other large cities Milano has traffic problems. Air pollution in the city can be bad, particularly in winter when cold still air from the mountains can trap the city's car exhaust fumes and cause a choking street level smog.

- Traffic jams are common despite over 20 road and rail rou[t] that can carry 15,000 people per hour. These commuters come from as far north as the Italian lakes.

- The home of two of the worlds most powerful football club[s] Inter-Milan and A.C. Milan. The media and industrial empi[re] that support these clubs look to European and world wide markets.

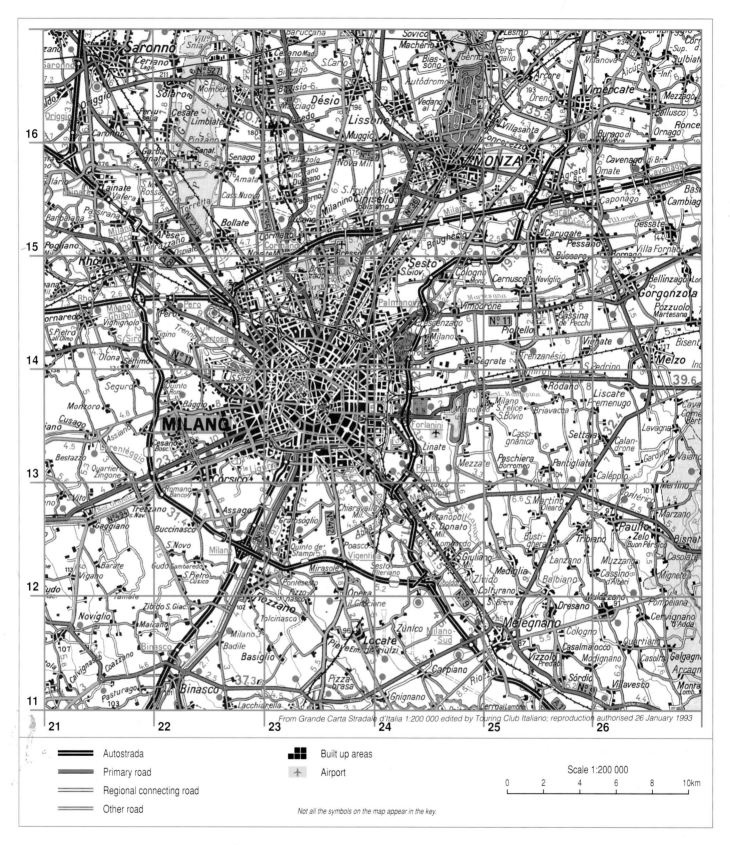

From Grande Carta Stradale d'Italia 1:200 000 edited by Touring Club Italiano; reproduction authorised 26 January 1993

Legend:

━━━	Autostrada	▪▪	Built up areas
━━━	Primary road	✈	Airport
━━━	Regional connecting road		Scale 1:200 000
━━━	Other road		0 2 4 6 8 10km

Not all the symbols on the map appear in the key.

...he network of roads that surrounds ...ilano link the Po valley cities to it.

...affic grid lock happens at peak ...nes making the 20 kilometre journey ...ross the city near impossible.

- Old towns like Gorgonzola, still a cheese making centre, show how the city was once surrounded by farm land.

- Monza has always been the home of Italian Grand Prix motor racing.

- Hot sunny summers contrast with winters that are colder and wetter than the rest of Italy. With the Alps and the Italian lakes close by, rivers feed south in to the Po valley.

Piemonte

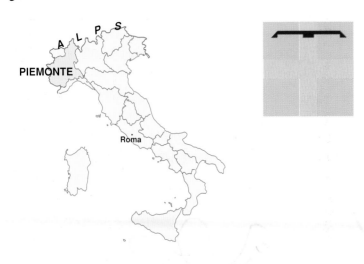

Torino, capital of Piemonte.

1. LANDSCAPE

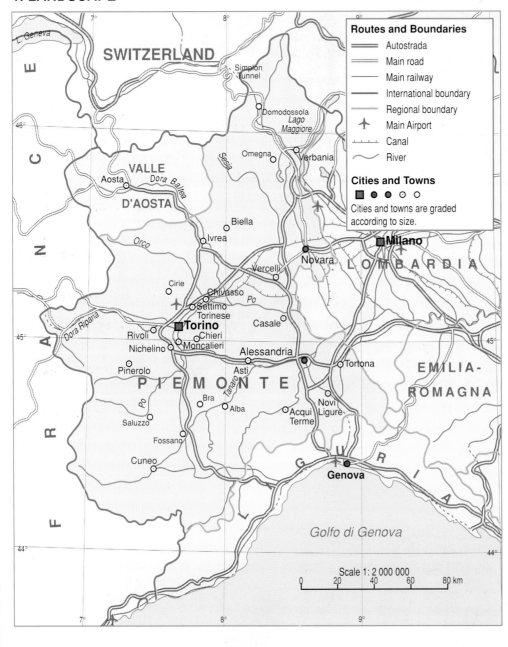

- On the mountain border with France and Switzerland, the region covers the upper part of the Po valley and Lake Maggiore.

- Tunnels carry road and rail links to neighbouring countries.

- Agriculture is important (wheat, rice, fruit and vegetables) and so is wine production.

- Hydro electricity from the mountain rivers helped start the car, clothing and textile industries.

- The car industry employs 90,000 people in the region.

- Winter ski holidays are an important tourist industry.

- The triangle of land between Torino, Milano and Genova has long been thought of as the industrial heart of Italy.

- The strength of local industry has helped banking and financial service become nationally important.

- The highest population density is around Torino, along the southern edge of the Alps and along the autostrada to Milano.

2. CLIMATE

- The mountains on three sides have cold snowy winters.

- The central valleys are often foggy in winter.

- Hot summers with regular thunderstorms.

- The spring and autumn rainfall maximum happens because depressions develop around the Alps that draw in damp air from the south.

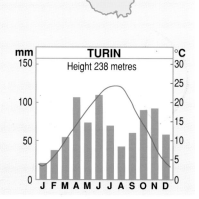

3. CHANGE IN EMPLOYMENT 1901 - 1985

Percentage employed by economic sector

Agriculture

Industry

Services

n.a. no data available

4. POPULATION

Population density
persons per square kilometre

over 1000
500-1000
200-500
100-200
25-100
0-25

Population of Cities and Towns
■ over 1 000 000
● 100 000-500 000
○ 25 000-100 000

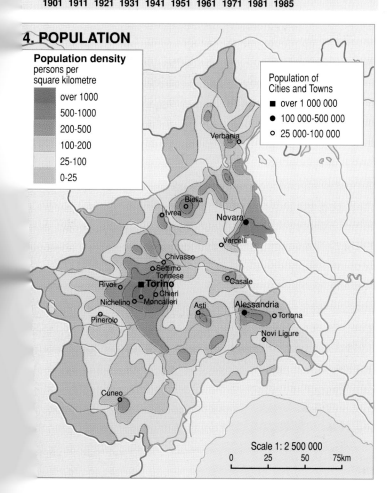

Scale 1: 2 500 000
0   25   50   75km

5. LAND USE

Woodland
Grassland
Extensive farming
Intensive farming
Uncultivated and Wasteland
Urban areas

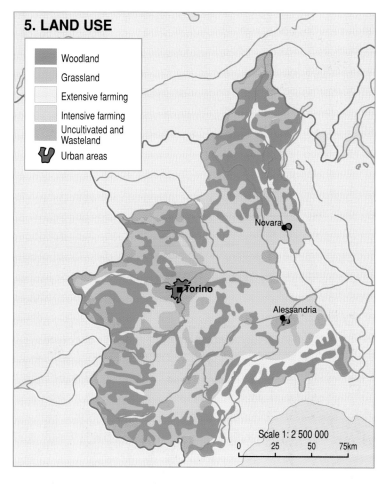

Scale 1: 2 500 000
0   25   50   75km

TOWNS AND CITIES

Torino (Turin) on the Po river is dominated by Fiat, half the regions manufacturing is found in the city.

Alessandria a major manufacturing centre and a route centre between Torino and the port of Genova.

Cuneo an agricultural market town near French border.

Novara has links with Torino and Milano, an important clothing industry and food processing centre.

Vercelli is Italy's main rice market near the growing areas near the river Po.

Domodossola is a developing ski resort with road and rail links to Switzerland.

Toscana

TOSCANA

Roma

Central Toscana, many towns in this region are built on hilltops, with small farms in the surrounding countryside.

1. LANDSCAPE

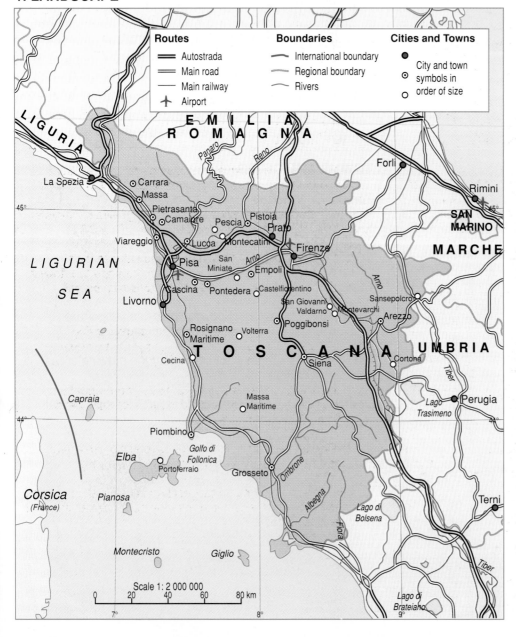

Routes		Boundaries		Cities and Towns	
▬	Autostrada	▬	International boundary	●	City and town
=	Main road	▬	Regional boundary	⊙	symbols in
—	Main railway	▬	Rivers	○	order of size
✈	Airport				

LIGURIA

EMILIA ROMAGNA

Panaro · Reno

Forli

Rimini

La Spezia · Carrara · Massa · Pietrasanta · Camaiore · Pescia · Pistoia · Prato

SAN MARINO

Viareggio · Lucca · Montecatini · Firenze

MARCHE

LIGURIAN SEA

Pisa · San Miniate · Arno · Empoli

Cascina · Pontedera · Castelfiorentino

Livorno · San Giovanni Valdarno · Montevarchi · Sansepolcro · Arezzo

Rosignano Maritime · Volterra · Poggibonsi

TOSCANA · UMBRIA

Capraia

Cecina · Siena · Cortona · Tiber

Massa Maritime · Lago Trasimeno · Perugia

Piombino

Elba · Golfo di Follonica · Portoferraio · Grosseto · Ombrone

Corsica (France) · Pianosa

Terni

Albegna · Lago di Bolsena

Montecristo · Giglio · Fiora · Tiber

Scale 1: 2 000 000
0 20 40 60 80 km

Lago di Brateiaho

CITIES AND TOWNS

Firenze (Florence) on the Arno river, in the Chianti wine growing region. Its many beautiful buildings date from its growth as a city state from 115AD onwards. The Dukes of Firenze dominated Toscana and the surrounding area. Tourism is important as are banking, financial services, jewellery, precision engineering, pharmaceutical and textiles.

Arezzo an agricultural centre with clothing, footwear and engineering important, good communications on the Firenze-Roma autostrada and rail routes.

Livorno (Leghorn) is a major industrial centre, shipbuilding, chemicals and oil refining, food canning with tourist centres along the coast.

Pisa is an old walled city with its famous leaning tower, good road and rail links help pharmaceutical, glass and pottery industries.

Siena is the heart of the Toscana hills and famous for its medieval streets. Major banking and agricultural centre with important processing food and confectionary.

2. CLIMATE

Local variations in the Mediterranean climate are clear in the graphs, Pisa is always warm, Firenze in the Toscana hills is in winter, but warmer in summer.

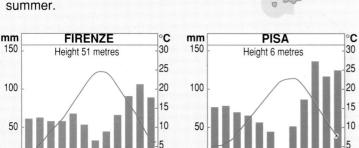

| mm | FIRENZE Height 51 metres | °C |
| mm | PISA Height 6 metres | °C |

3. CHANGE IN EMPLOYMENT 1901 - 1985

Percentage employed by economic sector

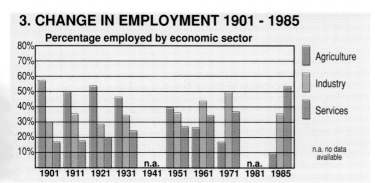

- Agriculture
- Industry
- Services

n.a. no data available

1901 1911 1921 1931 1941 1951 1961 1971 1981 1985

4. POPULATION

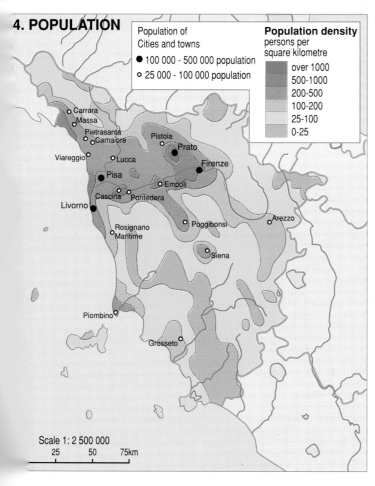

Population of Cities and towns
- ● 100 000 - 500 000 population
- ○ 25 000 - 100 000 population

Population density persons per square kilometre
- over 1000
- 500-1000
- 200-500
- 100-200
- 25-100
- 0-25

Carrara
Massa
Pietrasanta
Camaiore
Pistoia
Viareggio
Lucca
Prato
Firenze
Pisa
Empoli
Cascina
Pontedera
Livorno
Arezzo
Rosignano Maritime
Poggibonsi
Siena
Piombino
Grosseto

Scale 1: 2 500 000
0 25 50 75km

5. LAND USE

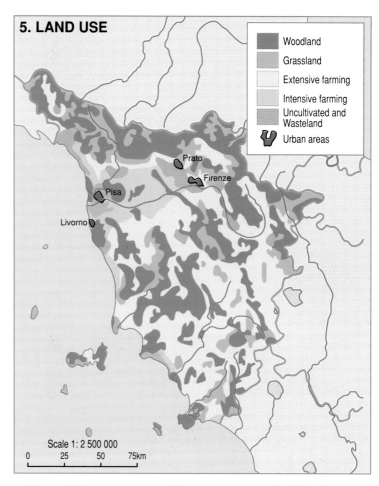

- Woodland
- Grassland
- Extensive farming
- Intensive farming
- Uncultivated and Wasteland
- Urban areas

Prato
Firenze
Pisa
Livorno

Scale 1: 2 500 000
0 25 50 75km

- Many of Toscana's towns and cities developed as small independent states. These are important tourism centres.

- Holiday companies encourage touring and villa holidays in the rolling hills and the Apennines.

- The population density map shows the link between communications and settlement. All of the important towns and industries have access to the autostrada and rail networks.

- An important farming area in Italy producing spring vegetables for the EC market, tobacco and high quality olive oil.

- The first area in the country to produce geo-thermal electricity, the region has a large number of textile and fashion industry companies.

- Alfa Romeo has a factory near Firenze and there are an increasing number of high technology companies.

- Agricultural employment has declined steadily. Industry has contracted, but service sector employment like banking and tourism has increased.

Sardegna

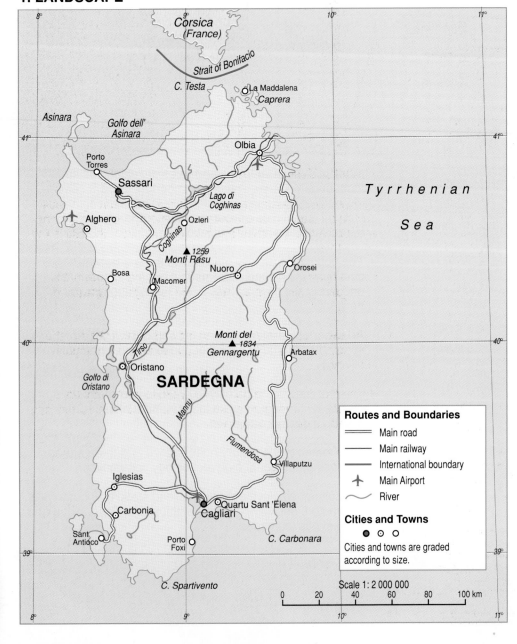

Cagliari in the south of Sardegna is the main port.

1. LANDSCAPE

- Isolated from Italy, Sardegna has developed its own economy and traditions.

- A mountainous island with open wooded countryside.

- Cagliari is the main city and port and there are a few large towns.

- Ferries to Roma, Genova and Napoli maintain the links with the mainland.

- Farming is important, with sheep and goats a common sight.

- Early spring vegetable crops produce for northern Europe.

- Little local fishing.

- Some coal mining, a chemical indust and oil refining.

2. CLIMATE

The two graphs show Sardegna's Mediterranean climate. A dry summer with a winter rainfall maximum. The sea breeze keeps the weather mild.

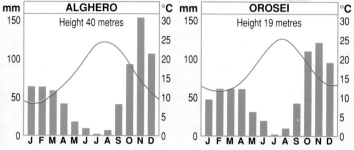

3. CHANGE IN EMPLOYMENT 1901-1985

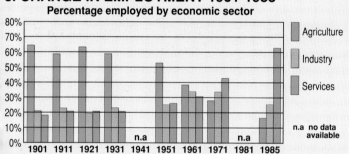

4. POPULATION

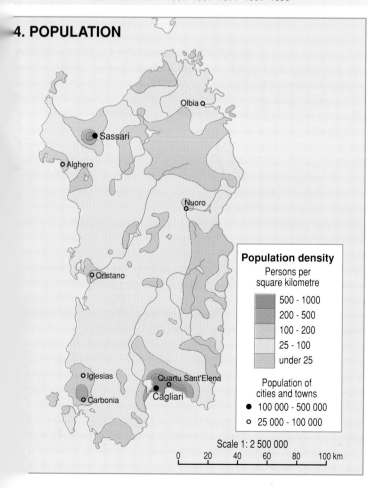

5. LAND USE

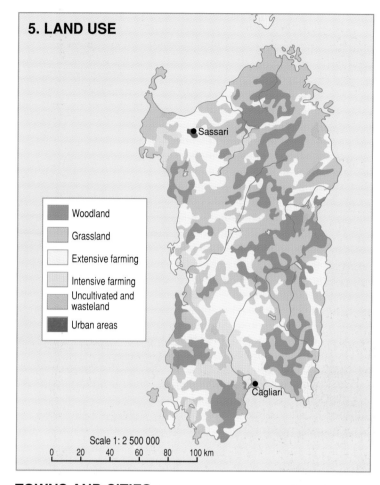

TOWNS AND CITIES

Cagliari is the largest city on the island, dominating a wide bay on the south coast. A major port facility with engineering and oil refining, chemicals and food production, the city is the administrative centre of the region.

Nuoro is high in the mountains. This farming centre is the chief town of the northern area, and has local government offices.

Oristano is close to the west coast and is the centre of the best farming area, with food manufacturing and chemical industries.

Sassari is the most important northern city with its own university, an important route centre within an area producing fruit and vegetables for export.

Puglia

Farming is important in Puglia; vegetables, interplanted with fruit are grown in irrigated fields protected by trees.

1. LANDSCAPE

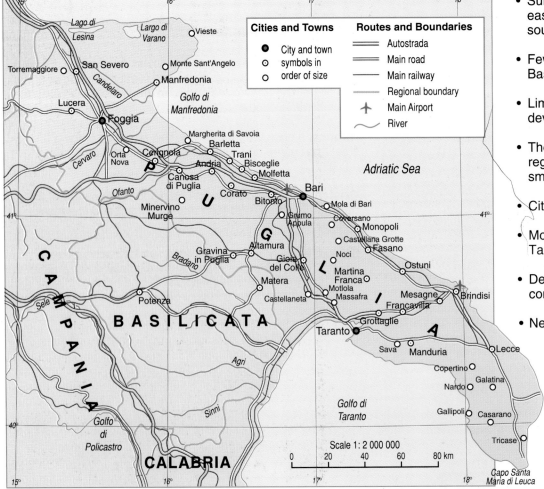

- Surrounded by the Adriatic Sea in the east and the Golfo di Taranto to the south.

- Few steep mountains except on the Basilicata border.

- Limestone rocks allow few rivers to develop.

- The second most important farming region in Italy, crops are grown on small farms.

- Citrus fruits are grown in plantations

- Modern industry has developed in the Taranto, Bari, Brindisi triangle.

- Densely populated rural villages are common near the coast.

- New autostrada are helping industry in Bari and Taranto.

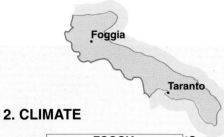

2. CLIMATE

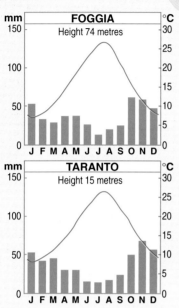

The mild winters help farming.
Summers are hot and dry, with
breezes from the sea.
Occasional thunderstorms and
the dry Scirocco wind affect the
region.
The south coast has a longer,
drier summer.

⟋WNS AND CITIES

⟋ari on the Adriatic coast, a busy ferry
⟋rt with petro-chemical and food
⟋ocessing industries.

⟋indisi on the Adriatic coast, a ferry
⟋rt and centre of the chemical and food
⟋cessing industries.

⟋ggia a route centre and market town,
⟋important food processing, textile
⟋ garment centre.

⟋ce a farming and wine making
⟋tre.

⟋anto a naval base and an important
⟋ for over 2,500 years. One of the
⟋est steelworks in Europe, chemicals,
⟋ processing and engineering
⟋stries are also important.

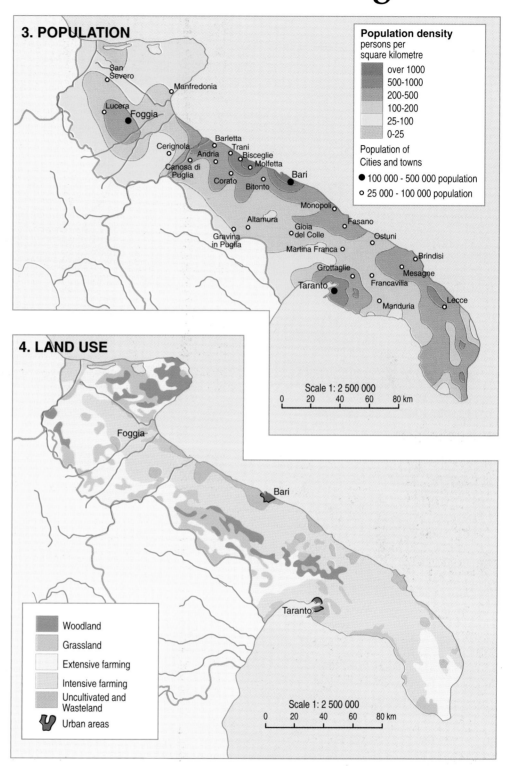

3. POPULATION

Population density
persons per
square kilometre

- over 1000
- 500-1000
- 200-500
- 100-200
- 25-100
- 0-25

Population of
Cities and towns
- ● 100 000 - 500 000 population
- ○ 25 000 - 100 000 population

Scale 1: 2 500 000
0 20 40 60 80 km

4. LAND USE

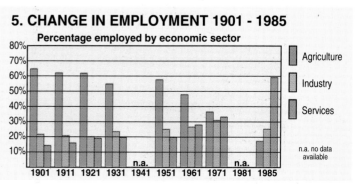

- Woodland
- Grassland
- Extensive farming
- Intensive farming
- Uncultivated and Wasteland
- Urban areas

Scale 1: 2 500 000
0 20 40 60 80 km

5. CHANGE IN EMPLOYMENT 1901 - 1985

Percentage employed by economic sector

- Agriculture
- Industry
- Services

n.a. no data available

1901 1911 1921 1931 1941 (n.a.) 1951 1961 1971 1981 (n.a.) 1985

Basilicata

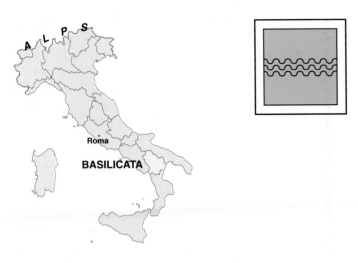

A region of small towns and villages, many of them high in the mountains, that appear to have been left behind by the modern world. The southern coast has a wide sandy beach dotted with quiet fishing villages.

1. LANDSCAPE

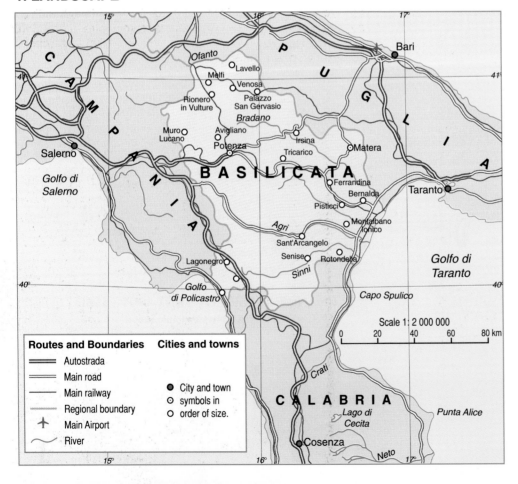

- Facing south on to the Golfo di Taranto.

- A narrow coastal plain with mountain that reach over 2000 metres domina the region. Steep sided valleys fill w flash floods during winter storms, ar dry to small streams in spring.

- The only Italian region where agricultural workers out number people employed in industry.

- The coastal area is important for winter fruit and vegetables.

- In the mountains small farms are looked after by older people, whilst younger people migrate to look for work.

- Industry is limited, but Fiat are building a new automated factory to the Autostrada at Melfi.

- Population density is one third of national average.

2. CLIMATE

With mountains over 2000 metres, the inland areas have cold winters, with high rainfall in the west. Summers are dry and hot, with occasional thunderstorms. The southern coast has warm winters.

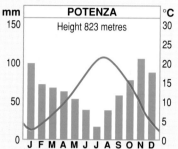

5. LAND USE

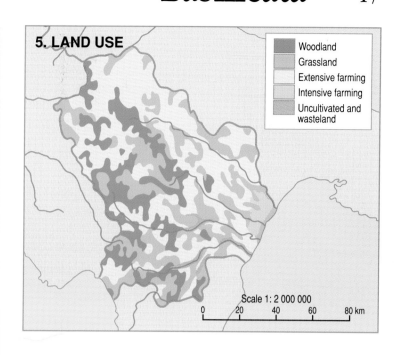

Legend:
- Woodland
- Grassland
- Extensive farming
- Intensive farming
- Uncultivated and wasteland

Scale 1: 2 000 000
0 20 40 60 80 km

3. CHANGE IN EMPLOYMENT 1901-1985

Percentage employed by economic sector

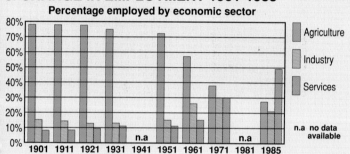

- Agriculture
- Industry
- Services

n.a no data available

CITIES AND TOWNS

Potenza is the regional capital. An important farming and market centre. Government development schemes have helped to establish small scale industry.

Matera, below, is one of the oldest settlements in Italy with a complete deserted cave village in the town centre, it has major tourist industry potential. Matera is a local market town with some small scale industry.

4. POPULATION

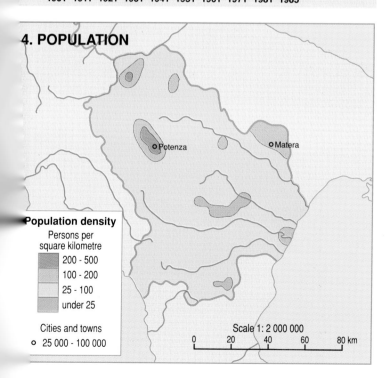

Population density
Persons per square kilometre
- 200 - 500
- 100 - 200
- 25 - 100
- under 25

Cities and towns
○ 25 000 - 100 000

Scale 1: 2 000 000
0 20 40 60 80 km

Acknowledgements
The publishers acknowledge the assistance of the following
in the preparation of this atlas:

Bedfordshire Education Service

Geographical Association Map Use Working Party

Fiat SpA.

The Marzotto Group

Prof. Vincenzo Arpaia
and
Prof. Maria Grazia Arpaia, Bari, Italy

Mr. Michele Arpaia S.P.P.S.
Italian Links Coordinator
Bedfordshire Education Department

Prof. Patrizia de Giradi-Franks S.P.P.S.
Bedfordshire Education Department

Prof. Gerardo Quatrale, Matera, Italy

Photo Credits:

Michele Arpaia
Citalia
Earth Images
Fiat SpA.
Goldsmith
Linden Harris
The Marzotto Group
Spectrum Colour Library

Map Extracts:
(pages 34-35 and 36-37)

Kompass Fleischman S.a.r.l., Bolzano
Touring Club Italiano, Milano